THE STORY OF THE PSALTERS

AMS PRESS
NEW YORK

THE

STORY OF THE PSALTERS

A HISTORY OF THE METRICAL VERSIONS
OF GREAT BRITAIN AND AMERICA

FROM 1549 TO 1885

BY

HENRY ALEXANDER GLASS

LONDON
KEGAN PAUL, TRENCH & CO., 1, PATERNOSTER SQUARE
1888

Library of Congress Cataloging in Publication Data

Glass, Henry Alexander.
   The story of the Psalters.

   1. Bible. O.T. Psalms--Paraphrases, English--
History and criticism. 2. Psalters. I. Title.
BS1440.A1G58 1972   223'.2'05209   72-1635
ISBN 0-404-08308-0

Reprinted from the edition of 1888, London
First AMS edition published in 1972
Manufactured in the United States of America

International Standard Book Number: 0-404-08308-0

AMS PRESS INC.
NEW YORK, N. Y.   10003

TO THE READER.

THE copy of "Tate and Brady," edition 1771, purchased for one penny at an old book-stall, was in excellent condition, bound in whole calf, and gilt-edged. More than three generations ago it had done duty in the earliest-founded church in the City of London, St. Peter's above Cornhill, and had been carefully used by "Mrs. Cobden on the other side," as appeared by a memorandum, no doubt by the careful beadle, or pew-opener. There was an indication that the lady had done more than join in the singing of the general congregation. Faintly written against the seventh verse of the thirty-fourth Psalm was the date, "Nov. 21, '79."

> "The hosts of God encamp around
> The dwellings of the just ;
> Deliv'rance He affords to all
> Who on His succour trust."

Who can tell now what was the deliverance which made the 21st of November a marked day in the history of the worshipper at the church of St. Peter ? Anno Domini 1779 was a year of wars and rumours of wars. Spain fighting us at Gibraltar, France in Jersey and the West India Islands, and the American colonists in the savannahs of Georgia. London was ill at ease by the news that sixty-six sail of the line and a host of other vessels were gathering at St. Malo, preparing for a descent upon England ; and the good citizens of Edinburgh were frightened half out of their senses by the appearance of the notable privateer Paul Jones, with "three small ships of war and an armed brigantine," in Leith waters. The Psalmist's songs of deliverance must have found an echo in her own experience when Mrs. Cobden used her Psalter "on the other side" of her parish church !

Pondering over the long-disused Psalter, the writer of the following pages felt a curiosity to learn more about metrical versions. The search after a history was fruitless. The nearest approach to it was " The Psalmists of Britain," * a descriptive catalogue of a large number of Psalm-versifiers, the great majority of the authors quoted being mere contributors to Psalm-literature in a metrical form. Whole versions, or complete Psalters, were only incidentally illustrated.

The present attempt is the outcome of the reflections suggested by the possession of the Tate and Brady Psalm-book of 1771, and the failure of the search after a succinct history of English Metrical Psalters.

The writer gratefully acknowledges his obligations to the Rev. Albert Watson, Principal of Brazenose ;

* " The Psalmists of Britain," by J. Holland.

Sir Robert Raper, of Chichester; Mr. W. L. Taylor, of Peterhead, who supplied many gaps from his fine collection of Psalm-books, and rendered valuable assistance in verification; the Rev. H. Elvet Lewis, of Hull, for his notes on the Welsh Psalters; the Rev. Brooke Lambert, Vicar of Greenwich; Mr. A. Boyd Cummings, of Philadelphia; the Librarians of the Philadelphia Library and the New York State Library; and to the officials of the British Museum, Sion College, and Lambeth Libraries, for their courtesy and attention.

VANBRUGH PARK,
  BLACKHEATH, 1887.

STORY OF THE PSALTERS.

CHAPTER I.

INTRODUCTORY.

IN the early Church psalmody appears to have been
a general practice. It was in the year 50 of the
Christian era—if we may credit Eusebius, as translated by the learned Archbishop Parker, in the
preface to his Metrical English Psalter of 1557 or
thereabouts—that " Philo, a Hebrew born, came to
Rome in the days of the Emperor Claudius, and
saw Peter the apostle, thus describing part of the
services in the houses dedicated to prayer by the
Christian people : ' Furthermore, they do not only
understand the ancient hymns of their elders, but
they themselves devise new to God's honour, whiche
they sing with all kinds of grave numbers and
rythmes in a comely honest manner, and with sweet
harmony.' And furthermore Philo saith, ' Our hymns
are so sung with us, that where one (a chanter) singeth

B

before one verse orderly and comely by observing the certaintie of his numbers, all the multitude beside, secretlye giving ear unto him, at the last sing together the latter parts of the hymns.'"

Gradually the musical parts of Christian worship were surrendered to the priests, or to an inferior order of clergy called Psalmistæ. Then the Council of Laodicea, in the year 363, forbade the laity to sing in church at all, except in certain simple chants—a prohibition which became unnecessary, as the Latin tongue ceased to be the language of the common people, and was used only in the ritual of the Church of Rome, or in the writings of the historian or the theologian. An order of monks made up for the popular abstinence, by instituting a system of perpetual psalmody. Relays of the brethren kept the song going unceasingly. Like the vestal fires, or the minute-bell of a Greek monastery, the music of the Psalm was never hushed by day or by night. In the diocese of Nismes, as late as the end of the fourth century, this kind of psalmody was known as the *Laus perennis* and *Psalterium perpetuum*.

The practice of metrical Psalm-singing in England and Scotland was for nearly three centuries after the Reformation *laus universalis* if not *perennis*. Never in any other country, not even in Judæa in its palmiest days, was the "Book of Praises" so widely employed in popular religious services as in the British Islands. For ten generations our forefathers lifted their hearts in praise and prayer in the rugged rhymes of Sternhold and Hopkins, or the somewhat more polished verses of Rous, and Tate and Brady. Although the poetry was for the most part beneath criticism, the versions had the merit of keeping as closely to the original Hebrew text as the vulgar tongue would permit ; and the rhymes, or jingles, as they too often were, conveyed the sense in simple language and easy measures. In a strange Anglo-Saxon garb the aspirations of the sweet singer of Israel found an echo in the hearts of Anglican, Independent, and Presbyterian alike. Critics might sneer at "putting David in fetters," but a people's joys and sorrows found expression in the homely verses, and hallowed even the jingles in their memories.

The object of the metrical Psalter was much nobler than the method and the manner of it. Next in importance to the translation of the whole Bible into the vulgar tongue, and declaring every man's right to read it and judge for himself, were the rhyming versions of the Psalms, which made the jubilant hymns of the Hebrew poets the songs of the people. Psalm-singing was a consequence of the Reformation. It carried the devout believer straight into the presence of his Maker and Deliverer, without the intervention of priest or Creed, and enabled him to shout in triumph—

"Ein' feste burg ist unser Gott."

It helped to lay deep the foundations of the religious liberty which now spreads more or less over the whole of Christendom. Wherever the early colonies of England were planted the Psalter followed. The first printed book in America was the "Bay Psalm-book," and the last of the stereotyped editions of Tate and Brady was used in the mission stations scattered over the four quarters of the globe.

The Reformers, John Huss, Jerome of Prague, the Bohemian Brethren, and Martin Luther, published certain of the Psalms in German metre for the use of the common people, "that priests might not be wanted." They did not attempt an entire Psalter; the Lutherans were satisfied with a selection of the Psalms interspersed with their hymns. The only entire metrical version which at all compares with the English was the French Psalter of Marot and Beza. Its history is interesting, not only on account of its superior literary merit, but because the tunes which accompanied it were adapted, in numerous instances, to the English Psalms, by Day, Este, and Ravenscroft, and still continue in use, having long outlived the rhymes to which they were set. Innocents, St. Michael's, and the Old Hundredth are now sung by "all people that on earth do dwell," in popular congregational worship.

"Clement Marot was the inventor of the rondeau and the restorer of the madrigal," writes Warton. It occasioned no little surprise when the French poet proposed to substitute his metrical Psalms for the *Chansons d'amour* of the French court, and bade the ladies of France place their

> ". . . doights sur les espinettes
> Pour dire sanctes chansonettes."

Whether it was on account of the growing spread of the new ideas awakened by the Reformation, or the brilliancy of the rhymes, the "sanctes chansonettes" leaped into fashion. The first edition of ten thousand copies was speedily exhausted. Princes of the blood, the king's mistresses, lords and ladies of the court, began to sing Psalms to the ballad-tunes of the times. Each one had a favourite out of the fifty which Marot composed. The Dauphin, as became a sportsman, chose "As the hart panteth after the waterbrooks," and Diana of Poictiers, "From the depth of my heart."

Writers of a later day, Isaac Disraeli among others, have found much amusement in drawing the picture of a dissolute court singing David's Psalms to fashionable jigs. But it is a fact, nevertheless, that the advent of Psalm-singing in the French court marked the commencement of a real religious awakening. Theodore Beza speedily completed the whole metrical version, which, with the tunes attached, received the sanction of the Sorbonne. The Psalter was dedicated to the King and the ladies of France, and was described as admirably fitted to the violin and other musical instruments: surely no reason why it should be considered as merely a fad of a volatile court. No one can take up the Marot and Beza by Jean Beaufoy, published at Lyons in 1566, or that of Jean Jannon, at Sedan in 1633, without seeing evidence that the Psalms were for the use of a devout Christian people, although with a good taste, that was national, they sang out of exquisite little duodecimos in calf or morocco gilt. The genuine devotional character of the French Psalm-book is evidenced by the fact that the austere Calvin adopted it, adding to it the Genevan Confession of Faith ; and its reforming tendency is shown by its being promptly added to the List of Heretical Books forbidden by the Church of Rome. Some other metrical versions in French have been published, notably those by Phillippe des Portes and A. Godeau ; but no French library can show editions of the metrical Psalms spreading over the centuries as in the British Museum and Bodleian Libraries, for the Revocation of the Edict of Nantes, in banishing the Huguenots, hushed the voices of the French Psalm-singers until long after the great Revolution.

As in France, the English metrical Psalter had a similar court origin. Thomas Sternhold was a Gentleman of the Privy Chamber to Edward VI., as Clement Marot was a Valet of the Bedchamber to Francis I. Sir Philip Sidney, to whom Ruskin gives a leading place as a Psalm-writer, was a courtier of Queen Elizabeth. Sir Thomas Wyatt translated several of the Psalms into English metre, published in 1549— the same date as appears on the first entire metrical version printed by Crowley. The Earl of Surrey, another courtier of Henry VIII., not only wrote a sonnet in praise of Wyatt's verses, but contributed other Psalms in rhyme himself. Alexander Montgomerie, perhaps the best of the earlier Psalm-versifiers, was a Captain of the Body-Guard to the Regent Morton, during the minority of James VI. of Scotland.

That the metrical Psalters first began to be used in palaces of princes is an evidence of the widespreading influence of the Reformation, rather than that of a fleeting fashion in court circles.

The English metrical Psalm was also an outcome of the early practice of popularizing almost every literary production by rhyming. It commenced in the reign of Henry II., when a paraphrase of the Gospel histories appeared in a kind of tetrameter iambic verse of fifteen syllables, with a moral poem upon Old Age in a similar metre; the syllables broken into two, the first line containing eight and the second seven, each alternate line rhyming. The minstrels had already begun to accustom the ear of the people to rhyme by using it in their romances; so that if the poet or the moralist wished to reach the multitude, history and philosophy were taught in jingling rhymes and simple though imperfect metres. Chaucer first elevated the practice into something deserving the name of poetry. The proverbs in use were, even in his day, almost always in rhyme. Contemporaneously with the first editions of Sternhold and Hopkins, Thomas Tusser published his "Five Hundred Pointes of Good Husbandrie" in rhyming couplets, in which he thus paraphrased the simplest article of religious belief as defined by St. Augustine—

"Since the world began there was and shall be still,
    Of human kinds two sundry sorts, th'one good, th'other
        ill;
    Which till the judgment day shall here together dwell,
    But then the good shall up to heaven, the bad shall down
        to hell."

Dr. Christopher Tye, organist to King Edward VI., published, in 1553, "The Actes of the Apostles translated into English Metre;" and his example of Scripture-rhyming seems to have been contagious, for in a few years many other books of the Old and New Testaments were similarly treated—canticles, proverbs, prophecies, and histories alike. Later on, Dod versified an Act of Parliament, and the practice culminated when a Mr. John Hopkins clothed "Paradise Lost," thirty years after it was first published, in a common metre, for the commendable purpose of "making Mr. Milton plain." George Buchanan rhymed the Psalms in Latin (for whose convenience perhaps scholars can tell); in turn, his Latin verses were rhymed into English.

As the poetry, if any, of the metrical Psalms was subservient to the rhyme, it is hardly fair to criticize the early metrical versionists from the standpoint of our advanced literary culture. Dr. Johnson, the prince of critics, declined to attempt it. "To have made men sing in concert, in the streets, or at their work, and merry or sad, on all occasions to tickle the ears with rhyme and touch the heart with emotion, was betraying no deficient knowledge of human nature." *

In England the old metrical Psalter is a thing of the past. It lingers in the Presbyterian Churches; but even among them there are signs that before long the common-metre rhymes of the oft-revised 1650 version of Rous will give way to the chant of the literal paraphrases. North of the Tweed the Rous

* Timperley's "Encyclopædia of Literary and Biographical Anecdote."

Psalter still holds as unchallenged a position as ever did Sternhold and Hopkins in England. Perhaps, instead of discontinuing the time-honoured practice, the kirks of Scotland will still further re-revise Rous, as the Marquis of Lorne did in 1877, and may eventually produce a Psalter which will satisfy the critics, and finally dispose of Dr. Johnson's dictum that no metrical version ever deserved other praise than that of "meaning well."

Since Mr. Holland compiled his volumes, although a considerable number of new metrical versions have appeared, none of them have come into use for congregational purposes, and they are already almost as much memories of the past as Sternhold and Hopkins, and Tate and Brady. It seems, therefore, to be a fitting time to sum up the history of the metrical Psalter, and place on record the long list of whole versions from Robert Crowley, 1549, to Digby Wrangham, 1885.

To have singled out all the contributors to metrical Psalm-literature during the last three centuries would have been an interminable task. Their name is legion. Queen Elizabeth composed "two little anthems, or things in metre," as well as a metrical version of the thirteenth Psalm,* as early as 1548, when Clement Marot was writing his "sanctes chansonettes." Since then, prince and peasant, lay and cleric, have produced their little "things in metre" innumerable. The difficulty would be to find among poetical writers on religious subjects those who have

---

* Ritson's "Bibliograph Poetica." Dr. Cotton says Ps. xiv.

not at one time or other tried their hands at the versification of a Psalm of David.

Even as regards the entire versions, a still further elimination of metrical Psalters might have been made without much loss; for, as far as popular use is concerned, the versions of Sternhold, Rous, Tate and Brady, and Watts stand out so far in advance of all competitors, that their history illustrates the whole subject of the rise, progress, and decline of metrical Psalm-singing in England. A proof of this may be seen in the subjoined table, showing the number of editions of some of the metrical Psalters now in the British Museum Library, and the periods in which they were issued :—

	1549 to 1600	1601 to 1650	1651 to 1700	1701 to 1750	1751 to 1800	1801 to 1868	Total.
Sternhold . .	47	206	102	120	105	21	601
Tate and Brady .			6	35	103	159	303
Scotch Version .			17	9	28	44	98
Watts . .				7	32	58	97
Wesley . .				2	8	3	13
King James .		8					8
Barton . .		1	4	2			7
Patrick . .			3	4			7

Dr. Cotton enumerates 309 distinct editions before 1700; the above table shows 355.

For the sake of completeness, however, all the versions and versionists have been described in their order of time. The full titles of their Psalters are followed by the first verses of the first and the twenty-third Psalms, and accompanied by short biographical or other notices. Should the reader

compare them, he will probably be surprised at the
ingenuity with which more than a hundred versifiers
have contrived to differ from each other, while for the
most part adhering very closely to the Authorized
Version of the Bible.

CHAPTER II.

THE STORY OF THE PSALTERS.

THE singing of metrical Psalms in the vulgar tongue first commenced in Scotland. The Wedderburns seem to have translated their versions from the German hymn-books—a practice adopted by Bishop Coverdale,* as will be seen in the comparison of a verse in Ps. lxvii.—

> "O God, be mercifull to vs,
>   And send to vs Thy blessing;
> Thy face shaw vs sa glorious,
>   And be euer to vs luifing."
>
> (Wedderburn, 1578.)

> "God be mercifull vnto us,
>   And send over us His blessynge;
> Show us His presence glorious,
>   And be ever to us lovynge."
>
> (Coverdale, 1583.)

A number of the Wedderburn Psalms had been translated into metre before the year 1546. George Wishart, who was burnt at the stake for heresy, sang

* Mitchell's "Wedderburns and their Work."

one of them on the night in which he was arrested.
Foxe, in describing the martyrdom of Adam Wallace,
1550, says, " He passed the night in singing, having
learned the Psaulter of David without boke to his
consolation." These songs are preserved to us in the
" Dundee Psalms," from the 1578 edition of which is
the following from Ps. xxiii. :—

> " The Lord God is my Pastour gude,
>   Aboundantly mee for to feid ;
> Then how can I bee destitute
>   Of ony gude thing in my neid ?
>   He feidis me in fieldis fair
>   To riuers sweet, pure, and preclair,
>   He dryuis me but ony dreid."

We have no evidence that Miles Coverdale's
Psalms were ever publicly used. Only one copy is
known to exist—that in the Library of Queen's
College, Oxford. In 1539, among the prohibited
books in the injunctions issued by Henry VIII., was
Coverdale's "Ghostly Psalmes and Spirituall Songes
drauen out of the Holy Scripture," in which he had
versified thirteen of the Psalms. "Would God," said
the bishop in his preface, " that our minstrels had
none other thing to play upon, neither our carters
and ploughmen other things to whistle upon, save
Psalms, hymns, and such godly songs as David is
occupied withal !" This is a specimen of his verse—

> " At the ryvers of Babilon
>   There sat we down ryght hevely ;
> Even whan we thought upon Sion,
>   We wept together sorofully.

For we were in soch hevynes,
That we forgat al our merynes.
And lefte of all oure sporte and playe;
    On the willye trees that were thereby
    We hanged up oure harpes truly,
And morned sore both nyght and daye."

The first complete metrical Psalter had gone out of
memory for nearly two hundred years when a copy
of it was discovered in the Library of Brazenose
College, Oxford.   Its date was 1549, and its author,
Robert Crowley.   He was a citizen of London, afterwards Rector of Cripplegate, in the ancient church of
which parish he lies buried.   Previously to his clerical
career he had been known as a man of parts as well as
a man of business—a printer, bookseller, and occasionally a preacher.   He edited the "Visions of Piers the
Ploughman," writing of it that "there is no manner
of vice that reigneth in any estate of men which he
[the author] had not godly, learnedly, and wittily re-
buked."   The moral tone which Crowley claimed for
"Piers Ploughman" was characteristic of his own con-
tributions to the literature of the times.   His teaching
might be summed up in the title of one of his own
metrical tracts—

    "Pleasure and Payne, Heaven and Hell,
    Remember these foure, and al shall be well."

We can readily understand how welcome an addition
he became to the clergy when Cranmer undertook the
almost hopeless task of filling the parishes of the land
with devout and competent incumbents in place of
the monks and priests who had been ejected from

their livings.   There is no record that Crowley's
Psalter was ever employed in public worship ; yet the
author's memory will be preserved in the annals of
the literature of his country as the first Englishman
who versified the whole of the Psalms of David in his
native tongue.

Archbishop Parker's Psalter (1557 ?), privileged but
not popular, was as little used as that of Crowley.
It seems to have had a private circulation.   Possibly
the reason why it was not put on sale was that Parker,
on his elevation to the see of Canterbury, dis-
countenanced metrical Psalm-singing as savouring
too much of the Puritanism which he detested.   His
verse, however, was better than that of his predecessor, as may be seen by comparing the following
lines from Ps. xxxvi. with the verses of Crowley
quoted in the description of the versions :—

" The words of his mouth : he unrightfully weighed,
In sleighty deceit : he they craftily lay'd :
Quite ceased he hath : to behave him aright ;
Good deed for to do : hath he driv'n from his sight.
All mischief he dreams : to advise in his bed,
From godly deserts : hath he turned his head."

Or the refrain of Ps. lxxiii.—

" Yet God is good to Israell,
to them of perfect hart :
Though wicked men : have here the sweete,
and good men feele the smart."

The next versifier of the Psalms " sang the rhymes

to his organ." Simple rhymes to simple measures
were united, and "common metre" took the place it
ever after retained as the most popular method of
"singing of the Psalms."

Thomas Sternhold, a Gentleman of the Privy
Chamber, 1540–9, whose heart had been touched
by the influence of the religious revival spreading
throughout the country, for his own solace at first,
translated some of the Psalms of David into English
metre. One day, while "singing them to his organ," *
in his apartments at Whitehall, absorbed in his devotional music, a delicate boy, who had not attained
his twelfth year, approached and listened with interest
and delight. Such strains, in the vulgar tongue, had
never been heard before—

> " O God, my Strength and Fortitude,
>   Of force I must love Thee :
> Thou art my Castle and Defence,
>   In my necessitie."

The little lad was the precocious Edward VI., who
was not satisfied until he had become better acquainted with the author and his work. In the early
part of 1549, not long before the death of Sternhold,
thirty-seven of his Psalms were published by Day,
dedicated to "the Most noble and verteus Kyng of
England, Fraunce, and Irelande, defendour of the
Faith, and in yearth of the churche of England, and
also of Irelande, the Supreme Hed." The pious
author added, "Trusting that as your Grace taketh

* Strype.

pleasure to hear theim song sometimes of me, so ye will also delight not only to see and read therein yourself, but also to commande them to be song to you of others, Thomas Sternholde, grome of His Maiesties Robes, wisheth encrease of health, honore, and felicitie."

Thus to Edward VI. belongs the honour of having first authorized a part of the metrical Psalter for public use. "Your Majesty," says William Baldwyn, in his dedication of the metrical version of the Canticles, in 1549, "hath already given a notable example in causying the Psalmes in fine Englyshe meter, by your godly disposed seruant Thomas Sternholde, to be song openly before your grace, in the hearynge of all your subjects."

Metrical Psalm-singing at once became popular ; but the accession of Queen Mary put an end for a time to all public practice of it. Before Edward's death the "Thirty-seven" Psalter had been succeeded by the "Forty-four," which contained seven added Psalms by Hopkins. In 1556 the Psalter had increased to the Genevan "One and Fiftie," Whittingham being the new contributor. It was this Psalter that was used in the church of St. Antholine's, Watling Street, where the practice of congregational Psalm-singing in church was first introduced, "the bell beginning to ring at five, when a Psalm was sung after the Genevan fashion, all the congregation, men, women, and children, singing together." Strype adds, "Immediately, not only the churches in the neighbourhood, but even the towns far distant, began to

C

vie with each other in the practice. You may now see at St. Paul's Cross, after the service, six thousand persons, old and young, of both sexes, all singing together and praising God."

Queen Elizabeth had not acceded to the throne more than twelve months when, by royal injunction, a new and entire metrical version of the Psalms was ordered to be prepared. In an early register of the Stationers' Company, a year or two afterwards, is the following receipt : "Received of John Daye for his lycence for pryntynge the residewe of the Psalmes not heretofore prynted, so that this maketh up the hole, iiijd." This "hole" version was completed in 1561–2, and published in 1564.

In addition to Sternhold and Hopkins, who between them contributed 100 Psalms to the version, Whittingham wrote 12, Kethe 10, Pullain 1, Norton 26, Wisdom 1, and 5 anonymous, total 155 ; five of the Psalms being duplicated.

The writers who completed the Sternhold Psalter will be chiefly remembered for their connection with the time-honoured version. Not, however, on account of the merit of their performances ; for, as old Thomas Fuller said, "They were men whose piety was better than their poetry, and they had drunk more of Jordan than of Helicon."

John Hopkins was a clergyman and schoolmaster in Suffolk, and is supposed to have been a graduate at Oxford in 1544. Little is known of him. Here is a verse of his from the original edition—

> " Why doost withdrawe Thy hand aback,
>   And hide it in Thy lappe ?
>   O plucke it out, and be not slack
>   To give Thy foes a rappe ! "

William Whittingham, a Puritan divine, was educated at Oxford about 1540, and afterwards studied at a German university. He was first heard of in connection with the Protestants at Frankfort, then as minister of an English congregation in Geneva, where he married Calvin's sister, and wrote the Psalms added to the 1564 version. He was Dean of Durham in 1563, his occupation of that office being chiefly remarkable for his encouragement of good music and his violation of monuments. He died on the 10th of June, 1579. Here is the doctrine of the Trinity in rhyme from his versification of the Athanasian Creed—

> " The Father God is, God the Son,
>   God Holy Spirit also,
>   Yet there are not three Gods in all,
>   But one God, and no mo."

William Kethe " made to run in rhyme " the Psalms that are attributed to him, during his exile in Geneva in Queen Mary's reign. He was Chaplain to the Forces under the Earl of Warwick in 1563 and 1569.* About 1561 he was settled as a minister in Warwickshire. He will always be remembered as the author of the hundredth Psalm, the only composition in the Sternhold and Hopkins Psalter which is still generally sung—

> " All people that on earth do dwell."

* He is also stated to have been Minister of Child Ockford, in Dorsetshire.

The tune to which it was set is also one of the few now used of the forty tunes that were attached to the original Psalters. The "Old Hundredth" was composed by Guillaume Franc, doubtless for Marot and Beza's Psalter; and appears in the Genevan Psalter of 1561, a copy of which is in the Library of St. Paul's Cathedral.

John Pullain was senior student of Christ Church in 1547, then thirty-three years of age. Queen Elizabeth appointed him to the archdeaconry of Colchester. He died in 1565.

Thomas Norton was born at Sharpenhoe, in Bedfordshire. He was a barrister-at-law. Wood, the historian, calls him a forward and busy Calvinist.

Robert Wisdom was presented by Cranmer to the rectory of Stisted, in Essex, afterwards to that of Settrington, in Yorkshire. Subsequently he became Archdeacon of Ely. He was classed among Precisians and Puritans, of one of whom Sir Thomas Overbury, who had no liking for them, said, " He conceives his prayer in the kitchen, rather than in the Church, and is of so good discourse that he dares challenge the Almighty to talk with him extempore. He thinks every organist is in a state of damnation, and had rather hear one of Robert Wisdom's Psalms than the best hymn a cherub can sing."

Few works, beside the Bible and Shakespeare, have been distinguished by a demand for concordances. In 1694 appeared a Concordance of the Sternhold Psalter, giving "the most material words in the Book of Singing Psalms for Parish Clerks." Until 1856 the old paraphrase was the only version which attained the like honour, when a "Concordance to the Metrical Psalms of the Church of Scotland" was published.

In Charles II.'s time Sternhold was printed in shorthand. In the British Museum Library are two curious little volumes in small 64mo (a half-dozen of them could be laid on the palm of the hand)—

The Whole Book of Psalmes in Meeter, according to that most exact and compendious Method of Short Writing composed by Thomas Shelton. Sold by Tho. Cockerill at the Three Legs and Bible in the Poultry.

The Whole Book of Psalms in Metre, according to the Art of Short Writing written by Jeremiah Rich, Author and Teacher of the said Art. London: sold by Samuel Botley, over against Vintner's Hall in Thames Street, and nowhere els.

Este, Day, and Ravenscroft, in the early part of the seventeenth century, issued Psalm and tune books combined, the former revisions of Sternhold, which were largely used in the churches. Thomas Ravenscroft's (1621) was entitled—

The whole Book of Psalmes, with the Hymns Evangelicall and Songs Spiritvall, composed into 4 parts by sundry Authors, with such seuerall tunes as haue beene and are vsually sung in England, Scotland, Wales, Germany, Italy, France, and the Netherlands, neuer as yet before in one volume published.

Among the musical contributors were Thomas

Tallis and John Milton, the father of the great poet.
It is from this and the other tune-books and Andro
Hart's Psalter (Edinburgh, 1615), that the old tunes
are taken which are still sung in Protestant countries.
St. David's is one of them; Dundee, French and
Martyrs are others.

The last edition of Sternhold and Hopkins, in the
Library of the British Museum (1828), is the Cambridge stereotype edition. It is bound up with a Tate
and Brady.

In 1556 the Wedderburn Psalms in Scotland were
superseded by the Sternhold "One and Fiftie," added
to the Genevan Form of Prayer. Parts of the contents of the "buik" are an almanac, a calendar, an
epacte (by which to know the age of the "mune"),
the dates of the Scotch fairs, etc. This was the
"Psalme Buik" presented to Mary Queen of Scots,
with "ane Bybill," by the citizens of Edinburgh, in
1561.*

Arrangements seem to have been made for bringing
out the first Sternhold Psalter simultaneously in London and Edinburgh. In December, 1561, "the Kirk
lent Robert Lekprevick, printer, twa hundreth punds
(Scotch money) to help buy irons, ink, and paper, and
to fee craftsmen for Printing of the Psalmes." It was
not, however, until 1564 that the collection afterwards
called the "Old Psalter" was completed. Added to
the Genevan "One and Fiftie" were sixty-eight from
the completed version of Sternhold and Hopkins, with
twenty-one by Pont and Craig, making up the number.

* McCries' "Life of Knox."

The following shows the variations between an English and a Scotch edition *:—

Authors.	English Edition.	Scotch Edition.
Sternhold . . .	40	39
Hopkins . . .	60	37
Whittingham . .	12	16
Kethe . . .	10	25
Pullain . . .	1	2
Norton . . .	26	8
M. . . .	4	2
Craig . . .	1	15
Pont . . .	1	6
	155†	150

Other Scotch editions followed. The earliest in the Library of the British Museum is—

1602.—The CL. Psalmes of David in Meter, with the Prose. For the use of the Kirk of Scotland.— Middelburgh, Imprinted by Richard Schilders, Printer to the States of Zeeland.

That of 1615 bore signs of considerable revision. The first verse of the twenty-third Psalm reads—

> " The Lord is onely my Support,
>   And hee that doeth mee feede :
> How can I then lacke aniething,
>   Whereof I stand in neede ? "

In 1634 Andro Hart, Edinburgh, published an edition, followed by another in 1635 by his " Heires ; "

* Livingston's " Scottish Metrical Psalters."
† Five duplicates.

and Robert Bryson, from his shop at "the signe of the Jonah," issued a third in 1641.

In 1693 the first American edition of Sternhold and Hopkins was published at Cambridge, Massachusetts.

In England, from the first, the Sternhold version ran through a fire of adverse criticism. Almost every scribbler thought he could improve upon it. But the few who tried their hands at a metrical version failed to produce anything more satisfactory. Lampooned by wits, Sternhold bore the brunt of the ridicule of Psalm-singing. A century after its publication and the adoption of Sternhold and Hopkins in public worship, on the eve of the glorious Revolution of 1688, a Cavalier poet wrote—

"Singing with woful noise,
Like a crack'd saints' bell, jarring in the steeple,
Tom Sternhold's wretched prick-song for the people." *

In this Victorian era, two hundred years still later on, there yet lingers among the older of our hymnal collections some of these "wretched prick-songs"—a sufficient reply to the irreverent criticisms of an irreligious age.

Following the Sternhold Psalms appeared the "Seven Sobs of a Sorrowful Soule," by William Hunnis, 1585. His seven penitential Psalms will be chiefly remembered by one of the additional hymns attached to them, perhaps the first metrical Evening Hymn composed after the invention of printing.

* Ed. Phillips.

A MEDITATION WHEN YE GO TO BED.

"O Lord my God, I wandred haue,
   as one that runs astraie,
And haue in thought, in word, in deed,
   in idlenes and plaie,
Offended sore Thy Maiestie,
   in heaping sine to sine ;
And yet Thy mercie hath me spard,
   So gratious hast Thou bin.
O Lord, my faults I now confesse,
   And sorie am therefore,
But not so much as faine I would—
   O Lord, what wilt Thou more ? "

Hunnis was " one of the Gentlemen of hir Maiesties honourable Chapell, and Maister of the Children of the same."

Alexander Montgomerie was a Psalm-versifier. It is a pity that he did not attempt an entire version. His verses are vastly superior, with the exception of Sidney, to the rhymes of his contemporaries of the sixteenth century. The Psalms of the Scottish poet might have outlived all the popular Psalters with their awkward rhymes and monotonous measures. The title of his contribution to metrical psalmody is—

The Minde's Melodie, contayning certayne Psalmes of the Kinglie Prophete Dauid, applyed to a nevv pleasant tune, verie comfortable to everie one that is rightlie acquainted therewith. Edinburgh: printed be Robert Charteris, Printer to the Kings most excellent Maiestie, 1605.

Compare the first Psalm in this collection with the specimens given later on of the various metrical versions, and the conclusion is obvious that the earlier poet has not been excelled, if equalled—

> " Blest is the man
> Yea, happie than,
> By grace that can
> Eschew ill counsell and the godles gates ;
> And walks not in
> The way of sin
> Nor doth begin
> To sit with mockers in the scornfull sates ;
> But in IEHOVAES law
> Delites aright
> And studies it to know
> Both day and night.
> That man shall bee
> Like to the tree
> Fast planted by the running river, growes ;
> That frute doth beare,
> In tyme of yeare ;
> Whose leaf shall neuer fade, nor rute vnlouse."

Another sixteenth-century versifier of the Psalms was Sir Philip Sidney, courtier and soldier, whose work was completed by

> " Sidney's sister, Pembroke's mother,"

and remained in manuscript until the year 1823, when it was printed by the Chiswick Press. Ruskin writes that there is more poetry in the seventh stanza of Sidney's version of the seventy-second Psalm than in the whole edition of Tate and Brady—

" Looke how the woods, where interlacéd trees
    Spread friendly armes each other to embrace ;
    Joyne at the head, though distant at the knees,
    Waving with wind, and lording on the place ;
           So woods of corne
           By mountaynes borne
       Shall on their shoulders wave ;
          And men shall passe
          The numerous grasse
    Such store each town shall have." *

Among the heroes of the Elizabethan age, who
were skilful alike in the arts of peace and war, was
William Myddelton (*Canoldrev*), who grieved that
his beloved Wales was hymnless while the new-found
song of praise rose from thousands of English and
Scotch worshippers. He was the elder brother of
Sir Hugh Myddelton, of New River fame. Shortly
after Captain Myddelton's return from the Azores,
where the English fleet had failed to intercept the
Spanish galleons, he wrote the " Art of Welsh
Poetry ;" and two years subsequently (1595), off
the island of Scutum, in the West Indies, he completed a metrical version of the Psalms, translating
from the Hebrew into Welsh, and " keeping as near
as he could to the mind of the Holy Ghost." Like
those of Montgomerie and Sidney, his metres were
too elaborate " to be song of al men," and little Wales

---

* " Rock Honeycomb." Ruskin adds, " ' Join at the head '—Sidney
thinks over the words, ' shall shake like Libanus,' till he imagines the
ears of corn so large that they shall touch, and close up together as the
heads of the trees do."

had to wait for nearly a generation before the metrical Psalm became part of its public worship.

Ainsworth (1612) better helped "the saints in the comfortable use of the exercise" by his almost countless annotations than by the facility of his rhymes. The version was, however, frequently used by the Puritans in their services, and was the first to enter into competition with Sternhold.

Dod's version (1620) received scant courtesy from his contemporaries. Wither wrote savagely of it: "Dod, the silkman's, late ridiculous translation of the Psalms was by authority worthily condemned to the fire." His Psalm-book, nevertheless, will always attract the curious, if only for its "Act of Parliament in Metre"—a work, doubtless, never attempted before or since. It was an "Act enjoyning a Public Thanksgiving on the Fifth of November."

> " Be it therefore enacted by
>   the royall maiestie
> Of our good King, and by his Lords,
>   divines and temporaltie—
> And also by authoritie
>   of this whole parl'ament.
> Th' foresayd poures and Commons all
>   assembled nowe present,
> That all and singular diuines
>   in Churches Cathedrall,
> And ministers in eurie Church
>   which is parochial :

Or other place, that is for vse
   of prayer knowne by name
In England's Realme or within
   dominions of the same,
Shall alwayes on the fifth day of
   the moneth of each November,
In prayers to Almightie God,
   give praise and thanks foreuer :
For this most wondrous happinesse
   in our deliverance ;
That so the same may be preseru'd
   in due rememberance."

Edmund Prys (1621) published a complete version
in a simple metre that could be sung by the people.
It is *the* metrical Psalter of Wales, for until recent
years no rival version appeared, and it still partially
retains its hold on the popular affection. The Rev.
H. Elvet Lewis says that ever since the Welsh
Psalter of Prys appeared, it has been one of the
chief treasures of Welsh hymnology. Many a simple
verse, rugged and massive in form, has been taken
up in great assemblies in unison, at first in slow and
halting tones, gradually rising and swelling, till at
last with overwhelming force it seemed to break on
the shore of ten thousand souls like the splendid roar
and rush of a mighty sea. This Welsh version, up
to the present time, has had a longer life than any
other. Sternhold has been completed about 250
years, Tate and Brady 140, the Scotch version now
counts 240, and the Welsh 270.

The Psalter which bears the name of King James

(1631) was in reality the "Lord of Stirling's," as it was called by Zachary Boyd. William Alexander, born at Menstrie, in 1580, was a young sonnet-writer who attracted the notice of the king, and being attached to the court, became his royal master's "trustie and well-beloved coadjutor" in a new versification of the Psalms. After the accession of Charles I., 1626, he was commanded by that monarch "to consider and revew the meeter and poesie of the work as far as it had progressed, and confer with the original text." Alexander "considered and revewed" the verses of the pedantic monarch so thoroughly that nothing of King James was left to be "conferred with the original." Possibly the reviewer was of the opinion of George Buchanan, the Latin versifier of the Psalms, who, being reproached that, when James's tutor, he had made the king a pedant, replied that "it was the best that could be made of him."

How far "our late deare father" was the author, as claimed by his son, Charles I., may be seen by comparing the verses of the 1631 edition with his manuscript, preserved in the British Museum. About thirty of the Psalms, finished or unfinished, are all that he is known to have versified, for before he made further progress—to quote the words of the Bishop of London, in his funeral sermon on the occasion of the death of the king—"God called him to sing psalms with the angels;"—let us devoutly hope in better measures than he employed on earth. Here is the commencement of the first Psalm in the manuscript—

" That mortail man most happie is and blest
   Qho in the wickedis consalis doth not walk ;
Nor yet in sinneris way doth stay and rest,
   Nor sittis in seatis of skornfull men in talk.
     But contraire fixis his delicht
      Into iehouaise law,
     And in his law both day and nicht
      To think is never slaw."

And part of Ps. xix.—

" The heauenis of michtie godd the glorie lett,
  And of His handes the workes spread out doth shou.
  Even so the nichtis do scyence (?) make us knou
  No wordis nor kyndlie speaches from them flou ;
  Yet without this thaire uoyce is understand,
  Theare beames and drauchtes (?) they with thaire speaches
    sou
  Thruoch all the earth and habitable land."

The king seems to have been satisfied with his work
as far as he had proceeded with it, if that meaning is
to be attached to a note on the page containing the
first Psalm : *"Dimidum facti qui bene cœpit habet !"*

Upon the appearance of the royal Psalter in Scotland, a zealous Presbyterian, probably David Calder-
wood, the historian, drew up, at considerable length,
" Reasons against the Reception of King James's
Metaphrase of the Psalms." King Charles, however,
was " fully convinced of the exactnesse," and enjoined
the Privy Council of Scotland to use "no other
Psalmes whatever." But when, in 1636, a new edition
was issued, it was evident that the objections had
taken effect, as the version was so much altered that

it bore only a partial resemblance to its predecessor. This new edition was authorized by the king "by open proclamation at the Market Crossess of the Head Burrows of this our Kingdome," and being added to the Prayer-book, an attempt was made to force it upon the Church of Scotland. An irresistible opposition was offered to it, however, and, in the troubles which soon overtook the king, all further efforts to introduce it were finally abandoned.

George Wither, in 1632, published his version. It was in lyric verse. He was one of a group of nine writers, headed by James I. and concluded by Zachary Boyd, who endeavoured to improve upon the Sternhold and Hopkins version. Day, Este and Ravenscroft altered many of the most rugged of the rhymes, without pleasing the critics sufficiently. Hence the attempts towards an entirely new versification. Wither seems to have published his first edition with some perturbation of mind, if we may judge from his preface: "If I have pleased my readers, I am glad; if not, yet I am glad; I have honestly endeavoured it. And (being assured my labour shall not all be lost) I will sing and be merry, by my selfe, in the use of this translation, untill others please to sing it with me; or untill a more exact version shall be produced and allowed." Poor Wither commenced as a Royalist lawyer, expanded into a major-general under the Commonwealth, and, after the Restoration, spent the greater part of the few years of life left to him in the Marshalsea and the

Tower. He received but scant courtesy from his
contemporaries. Getting a patent for his Psalms
from Charles I., the Stationers' Company fought
against his privilege before the Council, when their
Lordships were good enough to " damn his patent," as
far as adding his Psalter to the Bible was concerned.
When he was afterwards taken prisoner during the
Civil Wars by the Cavaliers, Sir John Denham, himself afterwards to be enrolled in the list of versifiers,
desired his Majesty not to hang him, " because that,
as long as Wither lives, I shall not be accounted the
worst poet in England." " The vice of Wither," said
one of his critics, " as it was generally of the literature
of his age, was a passion for ingenious turns and un-
expected conceits, which bear the same relation to
beautiful thoughts that plays upon words do to true
wit."

George Sandys (1635) was a poet, " ingenious and
learned," said Dryden, " the best versifier of a former
age." Addison acknowledged the benefit he received
by the study of his style. His version was " set to
new tunes for private devotion," and must have
been a solace to many readers, as well as to his
royal master Charles I. when he was a prisoner in
Carisbrooke Castle.

The Puritan writer of the Rotterdam version (1638)
very rightly thought that the following and other
verses in the Sternhold collection " called for amend-
ment : "—

D

> "Lord, when wilt Thou amend this geare?
>   Why dost Thou stay and pause?
> O rid my soule, my only deare,
>   Out of these Lions clawes."

(Ps. xxxv.)

> "O God, break Thou their teeth at once
>   Within their mouthes throughout,
> The tuskes that in their great jawbones
>   Like Lions whelpes hang out."

He claimed for his version a "tolerable smoothness," and that is all that could be said in its favour.

Another version of the same date, "conferred with the Hebrew Veritie," will be chiefly remembered on account of the disputes concerning its authorship. It was written either by Richard Brathwaite or Richard Burnaby. Possibly the writer was not anxious to prove himself the author of a Psalter commencing with the lines—

> "Blest is the man, whose walks are cleer
>   From wicked counsells aire."

The Bay Psalm-book, printed in America, 1640, was hopelessly bad. Quotations from it have afforded amusement to almost all writers on metrical psalmody. How far the critics were justified will be seen by the following "plaine" translations, as they are called in the preface :—

> "Like as the hart panting doth bray
>   after the water brooks,
> even in such wise, o God, my soule
>   after Thee panting looks."

(Ps. xlii. 1.)

> " I as a stranger am become
>   unto my bretherren,
>   and am an aliant unto
>   my mother's childerren."
>
> (Ps. lxix. 8.)

> " Prayse yee the Lord, o to the Lord
>   give thanks for good is Hee :
>   for His mercy continued is
>   to perpetuitie."
>
> (Ps. cvi. 1.)

> " And sayd, He would them waste ; had not
>   Moses stood (whom He chose)
>   'fore Him i'th breach ; to turne His wrath
>   lest that He should waste *those*."
>
> (Ps. cvi. 23.)

The Minister of St. Martin's, Leicester, Mr. William Barton, wrote a version in 1644, and had it printed by order of Parliament, and sold "at the Brazen Serpent, in St. Paul's Church Yard." According to the testimonials of his friends, his translations are " sweet," " exact," " apt," " excellent," " exquisite," and " elaborate ; " but they almost immediately came into competition with the famous " Mr. Rous his Psalms," and, after a struggle, gallantly maintained by Mr. Barton, the original versifier of the Scotch Psalter won the victory. Barton, however, always claimed that the version was " mostwhat " composed out of " mine and Mr. Rous's."

Francis Rous, the "old illiterate Jew of Eton," as he

was maliciously called by the Royalists, was the next versifier. In 1643 the Assembly of Divines, sitting at Westminster, were desired by Parliament to consider the subject of psalmody. They took up a recent version made by Francis Rous, read it over, and suggested sundry amendments. While it was still under consideration, in 1644, appeared an Ordinance of the Lords and Commons, substituting for the Book of Common Prayer a "Directory for the Publique Worship of God." One of the concluding ordinances was " *Of Singing of Psalmes :*" " It is the duty of Christians to praise God publiquely by singing of Psalmes in the Congregation, and also privately in the Family. In singing of Psalmes, the voice is to be gravely and humbly ordered : but the chief care must be to sing with Understanding and with Grace in the heart, making melody unto the Lord. That the whole Congregation may joyn herein, every one that can read is to have a Psalm-Book, and all others not disabled by age or otherwise are to be exhorted to learn to reade. But for the present, when many of the Congregation cannot read, it is convenient that the Minister, or some other fit person appointed by him and the other ruling officers, doe reade the Psalmes, line by line, before the singing thereof."

The Assembly sent up the amended Rous version to the House of Commons, November 14, 1645, making report : " Whereas, the Honourable House of Commons, by an Order bearing date November 20, 1643, have recommended the Psalms published by Mr. Rous, to the consideration of the Assembly of Divines, the Assembly has caused them to be carefully perused, and as they are now altered and amended do approve them, and humbly conceive they may be useful and profitable to the Church, if they may be permitted to be publicly sung."

The debates in Parliament spread over two or three years, and great opposition to the decision of the Assembly was raised in the House of Lords, caused by their preference for the version of Mr. Barton, whose Psalms were sent to the House of Commons, backed by a resolution recommending their consideration. They were returned, however, with reasons for not entertaining the proposition, the chief of which was that they were already committed to Mr. Rous. During the contentions between Lords and Commons, some of the Scotch delegates in the Assembly of Divines recommended the adoption of the version made by Mr. Zachary Boyd, with no better success. At last, on April 16, 1646, Mr. Knightly carried the Psalms to the Lords for concurrence, when the order for the singing of "Mr. Rous his Psalms" throughout the kingdom of England, dominion of Wales, and town of Berwick, was finally consented to.

The present Scotch Psalter (1650) is the revised version of the Assembly of Divines at Westminster, which, after still further revision, was enjoined to be used in the kirk by public authority. " It was then," says an anonymous writer, "the concurrent judgment of the Churches, that nothing ought to be sung in public worship but those Psalms, Hymns, and Spiritual

Songs which God has provided His Church with in the Inspired Word." That judgment has prevailed in the Church of Scotland long after hymnal collections had superseded the use of the Psalters in England.

Forty eminent and representative English Non-conformist divines subsequently adopted the Scotch adaptation of Mr. Rous, as they thought it "came nearer to the original of any that they had seen, and ran with such a fluent sweetness that they could not but recommend it." Undoubtedly the Scotch is one of the best of the old popular versions. With all its defects, there is a ring about it which we do not find in Tate and Brady, and a smoothness which was not a characteristic of Sternhold and Hopkins. It is difficult for Englishmen to realize how much the Rous Psalter entered into the religious and social life of the Scotch people. Wherever they went they took their psalm-book with them, and while Tate and Brady was slowly vanishing from sleepy parish churches in English rural districts, the sturdy Presbyterian might here and there be still heard shouting his Psalms with as great vigour as ever. Mrs. Oliphant, in her " Life of Irving," says, " Whenever his friends and followers sang the praises of God, it was that rugged version of the Psalms of David which we in Scotland know from our cradles, and, all poetic considerations out of the question, cherish to our graves. Those rugged measures by turns grand in their simplicity, by turns harsh and unmelodious, as only translated lyrics can be, which cheered the death-passion of the Covenanter, and which Carlyle, with an almost fantastic loyalty (in rebellion), puts in the mouths of his mediæval monks, Irving, in actual reality, put into the mouths of his English followers."

After the Restoration and the ejectment of the two thousand ministers, the English edition of Rous naturally fell into disuse. As an authorized version, it was not to be expected that the restored Church would suffer it to supersede the Sternhold Psalter, hallowed by old associations. Even the Dissenters neglected the Rous Psalter in its English form. Psalm-singing was no longer universal. In the early days of the Commonwealth, the general use of the metrical Psalter was evidenced by the fact that in 1644, at a grand banquet given to members of Parliament in Guildhall, the feast was ended with singing the sixty-seventh Psalm, Dr. Burgess giving it out a line at a time. In 1710 the practice of Psalm-singing had so far gone out of use in Nonconformist Churches, that it is stated of the songless Church, meeting in Devonshire Square, that disputes arose about congregational psalmody, which resulted in a compromise. After the morning service, those who objected to the 'unchristian infection" retired, and they who remained joined in singing one or more appropriate hymns.*

The New England Psalm-book (1650) was an American version of Rous, intended to take the place of the unsatisfactory Bay Psalm-book. It was largely used in the American colonies for more than

* Pike's "Ancient Meeting-Houses."

a century afterwards ; for no poet appeared who could improve upon its versification.

Cotton Mather's blank-verse Psalter, in the early part of the eighteenth century, was inferior even to the rhymes of Peter Foulger of Nantucket, the grandfather of Benjamin Franklin. The Quaker schoolmaster thus warned the rulers in his country not to " meddle with God's worship "—

" And I am not alone herein ; there's many hundreds more
    That have for many years ago spoke much upon that score.
    Indeed, I really believe, it's not your business
    To meddle with the Church of God in matters more or
        less." *

Mr. John White, the " Patriarch of Dorchester," was one of the ministers who sat in Council to decide which was to be the authorized Commonwealth Psalter. He was not a competitor for the honour, and his prudence will be commended by the reader when his version (1655) is examined and compared with Rous or Barton.

Dr. Roberts, a Presbyterian divine, and a leading member of the Assembly, also produced a Psalter in 1675, and failed to show any marked improvement upon his predecessors.

The Bishop of Chichester's (1651) was a praiseworthy attempt to get rid of "the unhandsome

* " The Looking-Glass for the Times."

expressions" in the old Psalters. "This worthy bishop," says Anthony Wood, "being at divine service on Sunday, in a certain church (at Langley, I think, in Bucks.), and hearing there a Psalm sung whose wretched expression quite marred the penman's matter, and his devotion, he did, at his return home that very evening, try whether, from the version of our Bible, he could not easily and with plainness, suiting the lowest understanding, deliver it from that garb, which indeed made it ridiculous. From one and another he passed on until the whole book was run through."

Dr. Woodford (1667), before he entered into holy orders, was a prolific writer, who at one time proposed to versify the first chapter of the Book of Genesis as a "History of the First Great Week of the World." In this undertaking he says he expected "great assistance from the Royal Society"! He does not seem to have had any scientific assistance in his edition of the Psalms; but they were of sufficient merit for the next poet on our list to consult him in connection with George Buchanan and George Sandys.

Sir John Denham (1668?), probably bearing in mind his savage criticism of George Wither, wrote a Psalter which was not published until long after his death. He was better entitled to the praise of "fluent sweetness" than Francis Rous. Here is a verse from his Ps. cxlv.—

> "O Lord my God, my songs to Thee
> Shall, like Thyself, immortal be!
> For ever I'll Thy praise express,
> And every day Thy Name will bless."

Miles Smyth (1668) and Richard Goodridge (1684) were scandalized by the defects of the old version. Smyth blushed to think how the metre had disguised so eminent a portion of Holy Writ, and Goodridge endeavoured to expunge many low and indecent expressions. " How rude," said he, " are the following! and taken from amidst the manners and language of the street!"—

> " Our soul in God hath Joy and Game."
> " There! there! this Gear goeth trim."

Goodridge certainly improved upon such lines as those he quoted, but not more than Dr. Ford (1688), who took for his model the Stirling translation of King James, and issued his Psalter "at the Three Pigeons, over against the Royal Exchange."

Dr. Patrick (1691) wrote his version with such "pious skill" that Baxter said "his holy affections and harmony hath so far reconciled the Nonconformists that diverse of them use his Psalms in their congregations."

Richard Baxter followed (1692), and immediately preceded Tate and Brady. He claimed to have done that which no man had ever done before him. By the use of brackets, his Psalms became long or common

metre at discretion. His bracketed version has an
odd look in the present day. Thirty years before,
Baxter had drawn up a reformed Liturgy. Had the
Presbyterians attained the supremacy in the two first
years of the reign of Charles II., as appeared not
unlikely at one time, instead of the ejectment of the
two thousand, the parish Churches might have
echoed with Baxter's Liturgy and Baxter's Psalms,
as appointed to be read and sung by royal authority!

The glorious Revolution of 1688 found the Church
of England firmly established, and the would-be
reviser of her Liturgy a persecuted Nonconformist.
More than a hundred editions of Sternhold and
Hopkins had been published since 1650, and its use
was well-nigh universal everywhere out of Scotland.
But there was a growing desire for an improved
version that might on its merits fairly be entitled to
supersede the Elizabethan Psalter.

In 1696 the version of Tate and Brady appeared,
which, by Order in Council, was allowed and permitted to be used in the churches. "His Majesty's
most obedient servants," Nahum Tate, the poet-
laureate, and Dr. Nicholas Brady, no doubt succeeded in improving Sternhold and Hopkins. Not
more, however, than some other versifiers. During
the period that intervened between the two Psalters,
many writers had advanced far beyond Sternhold in
poetic feeling and smoothness of the rhyme. Compare the first verse of the eighty-fourth Psalm of

Milton and Rous with those of Tate and Brady, and the latter is far from showing any superiority :—

> "How lovely are Thy dwellings fair,
>   O Lord of Hosts; how dear
> Thy pleasant tabernacles are,
>   Where Thou dost dwell so near!
>
> "My soul doth long, and almost die
>   Thy courts, O Lord, to see;
> My heart and flesh aloud do cry,
>   O living God, for Thee!"
>
> > (Milton, 1608–1674.)

> "How lovely is Thy dwelling-place,
>   O Lord of Hosts, to me!
> The tabernacles of Thy grace
>   How pleasant, Lord, they be!
>
> "My thirsty soul longs veh'mently,
>   Yea, faints Thy courts to see;
> My very heart and flesh cry out,
>   O living God, for Thee!"
>
> > (Rous, 1579–1658.)

> "O God of Hosts, the mighty Lord,
>   How lovely is the place,
> Where Thou, enshrin'd in Glory, shew'st
>   The brightness of Thy face!
>
> "My longing soul faints with desire
>   To view Thy blest abode;
> My panting heart and flesh cry out
>   For Thee, the living God!"
>
> > (Tate and Brady, 1696.)

The new version failed at first to make any impression upon the continued use of the old familiar rhymes. It was immediately attacked by the critics, who accused its authors of "rebelling against King David, and murdering his Psalms." Its zealous defenders had to engage in a polemical warfare. "A True Son of the Church of England," in a pamphlet published in 1698, alluding to the charge that the sense was frequently sacrificed to the exigencies of the rhyme, wrote, "Cavillers and objectors say that these New Psalms are too Poetical (?), and yet I am certain that none of them are more poetical than the original, or have bolder Expressions or more lofty and exalted Metaphors, or more lively Flights of Fancy, than those of David." A less flattering defence was that the version, "though not excellent, was not intolerable."

Only two or three of Tate and Brady's Psalms survive in our popular hymnal collections; but possibly one verse, wedded to Spöhr's music, is likely to be immortal—

> "As pants the hart for cooling streams,
>   When heated in the chace;
>   So longs my soul, O God, for Thee,
>   And Thy refreshing grace."

The version never even succeeded in entirely supplanting that of Sternhold and Hopkins. The nineteenth century was nearly reached before the former distanced its competitor; and not long after both became reminiscences of the past.

Like Sternhold and Rous, the Tate and Brady

version was subject to much revision.*   In fact, some of the Psalms were versified by other authors.   This will account for the Tate and Brady first psalm, as familiarly known, being different to that of the original and suppressed edition.   The "scoffing crew" in the 1696 Psalm-book was eliminated in the lines—

> " How blest is he who ne'er consents
>   By ill advice to walk ;
> Nor stand in sinners' ways, nor sits
>   Where men profanely talk."

This verse has become historical in the well-known anecdote of Lord Palmerston and Wilberforce, then Bishop of Oxford.   They were staying in a country house one Sunday, when the bishop elected to walk to church.   It came on to rain, and as Palmerston passed him in the carriage, a shout was heard, " How blest the man who ne'er consents, by ill advice to *walk !* "   Always ready with a repartee, the bishop promptly responded, " Nor *sits* where men profanely talk."

Possibly the Tate and Brady version has suggested more humorous quotation than even Sternhold and Hopkins, and the Bay Psalm-book.   A reading-party of Oxford men, as late as thirty years since, with vivid recollections of a party of old dowagers, who used to spend their time in discussing their neighbours, were nearly convulsed as they listened in Dolgelly parish church to the singing of Ps. xli. 6—

---

* The late Provost of Eton, Dr. Hawtrey, used to say that he had heard in his youth that Dryden revised Tate and Brady, and that to him are due the few poetic touches.

" Suppose they formal visits make,
    'Tis all but empty show ;
They gather mischief in their hearts,
    And vent it where they go."

Was it inexcusable, when two friends were listening to an illogical sermon, for one of them to pass his Psalter to the other, marked against Ps. xlix. 13 ?—

" How great their folly is, who thus
    Absurd conclusions make !
And yet their children, unreclaim'd,
    Repeat the gross mistake."

That " Ancient Presbyter of the Church of England," Luke Milbourne (1698), quickly followed upon Tate and Brady, and was the last versifier of the seventeenth century. It was of him that Pope wrote, " Dulness is sacred in a sound divine." But the critics never treated fairly the metrical translators of the Psalms.

If Pope satirized Milbourne, Swift's ridicule of Daniel Burgess (1714) was yet more bitter. The popular Nonconformist minister was accused of mixing up with his oratory " unction with incoherence and ribaldry." His Psalms fared little better with some of his reviewers, if we may judge from the allusion in Billingsley's preface to " little impertinent criticisms."

Sir Richard Blackmore (1721) improved the versi-

fication of the English Psalter. As a literary production, his version possessed considerable merit,
although it did not escape the satire of the wits of
the period. Pope, in the "Dunciad," wrote—

> "But far o'er all, sonorous Blackmore's strain;
>   Walls, steeples, skies, bray back to him again.
>
> ,   .   .   .
>
>   All hail him victor in both gifts of song,
>   Who sings so loudly and who sings so long."

In 1719 the Dissenters recovered their capacity for
Psalm-singing in the "Imitation of the Psalms in the
Language of the New Testament," by Dr. Isaac Watts.
Its poetical diffuseness gave a new appearance to
the Book of Praises. The Psalms became hymns, and
not mere rhyming paraphrases of the Hebrew poets.
What they lost in literalness they gained in fervour.
It soon became apparent that the days of the old
"closely-fitting" Psalms were numbered, and that the
effort in future would be to produce the Psalms
"newly dressed." To use his own language, Watts
was the first who "brought down the royal author
into the common affairs of the Christian life, and led
the Psalmist of Israel into the Church of Christ without anything of a Jew about him." He accomplished
his object, however, by completely changing the
character of the Psalms. "Watts was almost the
inventor of hymns in our language," wrote James
Montgomery.

It is remarkable how instantly Watts's songs

gained the ear of the people. Pike says that four thousand copies of Watts's Psalms were sold in the first year of its production ; and when he joined his collection of hymns with it, the "circulation of these sacred pieces far exceeded the bounds of human comprehension." The same writer adds, in another place, that Watts's "Poems for Children" were even more popular, and were "dispersed by millions." In fact, no "closely fitting" metrical translation of the Psalms could ever reach the height of the fresh inspiration of a Christian poet. What verses of Sternhold, or Rous, or Tate and Brady, could bear comparison with such hymns as "When I survey the wondrous cross" ?

Yet Watts did not escape the fierce criticisms which followed after all other Psalm-versifications. Bradbury contemptuously spoke of his verses as "garblings, manglings, and transformings ; " and was said once to have stopped a clerk who was giving out one of his hymns, with "Let us have none of Mr. Watts's whims."

Many of the subsequent versionists used the example of liberty set them by Dr. Watts very freely. David was sacrificed to doctrine, rather than enlarged in the spirit of Christianity, as claimed by Kit Smart. The following shows what a wide range was taken by some of the authors :—

E

Date.	Author.	Object.
1754	Wheatland and Silvester	Translated into heroic verse in as liberal a manner as rhyme and metre would allow.
1765	Smart	Put evangelical matter in the place of expressions that seem to be contrary to Christ.
1773	Maxwell	Substituted the sacrifice of Christ for all allusions to "brutal sacrifices."
1776	Barclay	Paraphrased according to New Testament interpretation.
1797	Winchester	Adapted his Psalter to Christian worship according to the doctrine held by Universalists.
1801	Cottle	Gave a connected train to the ideas of the Psalm when they were disjointed.
1811	Goode	Adapted his version to the Christian dispensation.
1815	Donald	Made the Psalms hymns of Christian experience.
1821	Woodd	Directed the mind to the life, death, and resurrection of the Lord Jesus Christ.
1824	Turner	Adapted the Psalms for the purpose of congregational singing.
1825	Sankey	Had an eye to the beautiful in Church music.
1828	Patullo	Adapted her version to all denominations of Christians.
1829	Wrangham	Suited it to general parochial psalmody.
1831	Bartholomew	Rendered the Psalms more applicable to parochial psalmody.
1833	Musgrave	Rendered his Psalms in different terms from those to which the ear of the many had been accustomed.
1833	Ducarel	Gave more connection and continuity to each composition.
1834	Lyte	Gave the spirit of each Psalm in such a compass as the public taste would tolerate.
1844	Feilde	Paraphrased for the inmates of a cottage.
1847	Irons	Trusted that Socinians, Arians, and Arminians would find no music in his version for their falsehoods.
1848	W. H. B.	Sought to develop Christian doctrines in strict accordance with those maintained by the Established Church.

Some of these versionists, if they did not murder

the Psalms of David, took very great liberties with them. The "Sweet Singer of Israel" was employed in aid of Calvinist and Arminian, Methodist and Presbyterian, with a recklessness which makes the reader of the present day stand aghast at the temerity of the rhymers. Mr. Irons (1847), in his metrical version, clothes his hyper-Calvinism in the language addressed to the "chosen people," as if the doctrine of election had been held by Moses, and had found expounders in the other writers of the Book of Praises. Winchester made David tune his harp to the glorification of the doctrine of the "final restoration." W. H. B. (1848) made the Psalmist develop Christian doctrine as maintained by the Established Church ; and Miss Patullo instructed him to sing so as not to offend "the various denominations."

But perhaps the most remarkable instance of using David with a purpose was that of Maxwell (1773). Full of the prejudices of his Church against instrumental music being employed in public worship, he tried to eliminate or explain away all references to the subject in his new version. How he succeeded will be seen by his paraphrase of the ninth verse of Ps. cxliv., "I will sing a new song unto Thee, O God : upon a psaltery . . . of ten strings will I sing praises unto Thee."

> " I'll sing a new song to the Lord
>   With my whole heart and tongue,
>   By me His works, His ways, His Word,
>   Shall cheerfully be sung."

Also Ps. cxlix. 3, "Let them praise His Name in

the dance : let them sing praises unto Him with the
timbrel and harp."

> " Let them their Saviour's glorious Name
>   With praises high advance ;
> And loud His mighty power proclaim
>   Who doth their joys enhance."

Finding it impossible to keep out the instruments
in Ps. cl., he ingeniously lays the responsibility of his
compelled references on the Jews. Ps. cl. 3–5, "Praise
Him with the sound of the trumpet : praise Him with
the psaltery and harp.   Praise Him with the timbrel
and dance : praise Him with stringed instruments
and the pipe.   Praise Him upon the loud cymbals :
praise Him upon the high-sounding cymbals."

> " As did with instruments the Jews
>   His praises high proclaim ;
> Let us our hearts and voices use
>   To magnify His Name.
>
> " As they with timbrels in the dance,
>   And instruments well-strung,
> Prais'd God, let us His praise advance
>   With well-tun'd heart and tongue.
>
> " Like cymbals let our cheerful tongues
>   His praises sound on high :
> And let our sweet harmonious songs
>   Transcend the lofty sky."

The " Bard of Methodism," Charles Wesley (1740),
kept the Jew out of the Psalms as successfully as
Dr. Watts. They became Methodist songs. John
Wesley, his celebrated brother, with an entire absence

of any false modesty, claimed for the poetical compositions of himself and his prolific coadjutor, that in them "there are no doggerel, nothing put in to patch up the rhyme; no feeble expletives. Here is nothing turgid or bombast, on the one hand; or low and creeping on the other. Here are no cant expressions, no word without meaning. Here are (allow me to say) both the purity, the strength, and the elegance of the English language, and at the same time the utmost simplicity and plainness suited to every capacity." *

Poor Kit Smart (1765), unhappy poet! was the only one of the versifiers of David who wrote a song *to* him. His metrical Psalter, like a hundred others, is likely never to be read except by the curious; yet, when freed from the necessity either of closely fitting his rhymes or enlarging them in a Christian spirit, and addressing himself to the object of his lifelong admiration, he rose to the occasion, and produced a poem which placed him in the front rank of the writers of his age. It seems almost incredible that the same hand that composed the rhymes of the metrical version, inscribed, with a key upon the wainscot of a room in which he was confined as a lunatic, the noble "Song to David," remarkable, not only for its intensity, but for its Miltonic sublimity. Surely the Hebrew poet never had a higher tribute than the lines in reference to the Psalmist's anticipation of the long-promised Messiah.

* Preface to the Wesleyan Hymn-book.

" Glorious the sun in mid career ;
 Glorious th' assembled fires appear ;
  Glorious the comet's train.

  .   .   .   .

Glorious the northern lights astream ;
 Glorious the song, when God's the theme ;
  Glorious the thunder's roar ;

  .   .   .   .

Glorious—more glorious is the crown
Of Him that brought salvation down,
  By meekness, called Thy Son ;
Thou th' stupendous truth believed,
And now the matchless deed's achieved,
  DETERMINED, DARED, AND DONE."

Till the end of the century, now and then a versifier still attempted the old-fashioned literal Psalters. Mr. Pike (1751) preferred closeness to the text to the rhyme ; Thomas Prince (1758), taking the New England Psalm-book as a model, endeavoured to find a nearer approach to the inspired original ; James Merrick (1765), whose Psalms were extensively used in Tattersall's editions, kept as rigidly as he could to the text ; and Boswell (1786) improved the metre of the Scotch version while retaining its literalness.

Not one of them, however, was popular in a national sense. More than a hundred editions of Sternhold and Hopkins were published between 1750 and 1800, and as many more of the version of Tate and Brady. The latter reached its culminating point in the first half of the next century, while the Sternhold sale diminished to nothing, anticipating a

similar extinction of Tate and Brady by compara-
tively a few years.

In the present century more whole versions have
been produced than in the two hundred and fifty years
which preceded it.   They have suffered the same fate
as the more ancient Psalters.   Hymnals have superseded them all.   Yet not a few of the recent metrical
paraphrases leave little to be desired as translations
faithfully reproducing the sentiments and rhythm of
the Hebrew Psalter, whilst clothing its songs in more
or less polished English verse.

Some of the most painstaking and satisfactory
versions of the nineteenth century will be found to
be by American writers.   Dr. Allen (1835) gives as
many as six original versions of some of the Psalms
—a metrical feast to the lover of the Book of Praises.
Professor Abner Jones (1854) renders his version in
various measures, divided according to musical cadences, the responsive lines being kept unbroken.
He retains the original compass of the words of the
prose versions, which he laboriously calculates in his
preface.   Here is his comparison—

Hebrew version, 150 Psalms, 5280 lines.				
Abner Jones	,,	5338	,,	
Rous	,,	8340	,,	
Tate and Brady	,,	8632	,,	
Dr. Watts	,,	9500	,,	(not complete)

As the object of this work, however, is to give a
history of metrical Psalm-books, and not a criticism,
the reader must be referred to the details of the
versions for a closer acquaintance.

No one has succeeded in the attempt to provide a new national Psalm-book to take the place vacated by Sternhold and Hopkins, and Tate and Brady ; nor has any single writer ever succeeded in making his mark on each of the hundred and fifty Psalms and anthems which constitute the collection called by the name of King David. An ideal Psalter would, perhaps, be a selection culled from the best versifiers ; * but what compiler, or number of compilers, could satisfy the requirements of the critics, and at the same time overcome the prejudices and meet the tastes of a nation ? And if an attempt to produce a generally accepted selected Psalter were successful, it would, after all, only become an accessory to the hymn-book. The hymn is now embedded in Christian worship, not only as an addition to the ritual of a cathedral, but as the only part of the service, in Churches without ritual, in which minister and people can unite with one heart and one voice.

* The author of "Anthologia Davidica" and others have attempted the work ; none of them, however, gaining the public ear.

CHAPTER III.

THE METRICAL VERSIONS.

THE following, as far as can be ascertained, is an exhaustive list of those who are, with few exceptions, versionists of the whole of the Psalms. Lowndes mentions versions by George Scott, Edinburgh, and James Neligan, Dublin. The inquiries for them have proved fruitless. Doubtless some metrical whole versions have escaped notice, and it may also be thought that if Bishop Hare's and the Tingstadius versions have been inserted, others of a similar character might have been placed in the list, notably the scholarly and refined paraphrase of the Rev. T. K. Cheyne, D.D. The Gaelic versions in Scotland and the Erse version in Ireland, appear to be translations from Rous.

Date.	Name.	Rank or Occupation.
1549	Robert Crowley	Rector of Cripplegate.
1557?	Matthew Parker	Archbishop of Canterbury.
1564	Thomas Sternhold	Groom of H.M. Privy Chamber.
1565?	George Buchanan	Poet, historian, and statesman.
1580?	Sir Philip Sidney	Soldier and statesman.
1603	William Myddelton	Soldier and naval commander.
1612	Henry Ainsworth	Puritan minister—Brownist.

Date.	Name.	Rank or Occupation.
1620	Henry Dod	" Silkman."
1621	Edmund Prys	Archdeacon of Merioneth.
1631	King James	James I. of England, VI. of Scotland.
1632	George Wither	Lawyer and major-general.
1636	George Sandys	Poet and traveller.
1638	Rotterdam version	Puritan divine ?
1638	Richard Brathwaite or Burnaby ?	Dep.-Lieut. county of Westmoreland.
1640	Bay Psalm-book	Three New England ministers.
1643	Francis Rous	Provost of Eton, and member of Commonwealth Parliaments.
1644	William Barton	An ejected minister of 1662.
1648	Zachary Boyd	Minister of Barony Church, Glasgow.
1650	Scotch Psalter	Rous, revised by Commissioners.
1650	New England Psalm-book	Rous, revised by " thirty-two learned and pious persons."
1651	Henry King, D.D.	Bishop of Chichester.
1655	John White	Minister of God's Word in Dorchester.
1667	Samuel Woodford, D.D.	Rector of Hartley Malduith, Hants.
1668?	Sir John Denham	Knight, author of "Cooper's Hill."
1668	Miles Smyth	Secretary to Dr. Sheldon, Archbishop of Canterbury.
1674	Francis Roberts, D.D.	Rector of Wrington, in Somersetshire.
1684	Richard Goodridge	
1688	Simon Ford, D.D.	Rector of Old Swinford, Worcestershire.
1691	John Patrick, D.D.	Preacher to the Charterhouse.
1692	Richard Baxter	Parish minister of Kidderminster.
1696	Tate and Brady	Tate, poet-laureate ; Brady, Vicar of Richmond, Surrey.
1698	Luke Milbourne	Rector of St. Ethelburga's, Bishopsgate.
1704	Charles Darby	Rector of Kedington, in Suffolk.
1714	Daniel Burgess	Minister of Church meeting at New Court, London.
1718	Cotton Mather	New England minister.
1719	Isaac Watts, D.D.	Independent minister.
1721	Sir Richard Blackmore	Knight, physician to William III.
1740	Charles Wesley	Methodist minister.
1751	Samuel Pike	Sandemanian minister.
1752	John Barnard	Pastor at Marblehead, New England.
1754	Thomas Cradock, D.D.	Rector of St. Thomas's, Baltimore, Maryland.
1754	Wheatland and Silvester	
1755	Francis Hare, D.D.	Bishop of Chester.
1758	Thomas Prince	Pastor of South Church, Boston, New England.

Date.	Name.	Rank or Occupation.
1759	George Fenwick	Rector of Hallaton, Leicester.
1765	James Merrick	M.A., a clergyman.
1765	Christopher Smart	Poet, or hack writer?
1767	Protest. Dutch Psalter	Consistory of Dutch Church, New York.
1773	James Maxwell	S.D.P., Glasgow.
1776	John Barclay	Minister of the Bereans, Edinburgh.
1786	Robert Boswell	Writer to the Signet.
1794	Tingstadius version	Professor at Upsal University.
1797	Elhanan Winchester	"Final Restoration" minister of the Gospel.
1801	Joseph Cottle	Bookseller.
1808	Thomas Dennis	Curate of Haslemere, Surrey.
1809	John Stow	A lay member of the Church of England.
1811	Wm. S. Towers	Private gentleman.
1811	William Goode	Rector of St. Ann's, Blackfriars.
1815	Robert Donald	
1820	G. F. Holford	Member of Parliament.
1821	William Coldwell	Geological surveyor and architect.
1821	Basil Woodd	Rector of Drayton Beauchamp, Bucks.
1822	James Montgomery	Editor, printer, poet.
1823	James Usher	
1824	Baptist Noel Turner	Rector of Denton, Somersetshire.
1824	Richard Mant, D.D.	Bishop of Down and Connor.
1825	Matthew Sankey	
1826	Edward Rowland	Retired timber-merchant, afterwards clergyman.
1827	John Maule	Doctor of medicine.
1828	Margaret Patullo	Scotchwoman of good family.
1829	William Wrangham	A tradesman of Louth.
1831	Walter J. Trower, D.D.	Bishop of Glasgow and Galloway.
1831	Alfred Bartholomew	Architect.
1832	Edward G. Marsh	M.A., Minister of Hampstead Chapel.
1832	Henry Gahagan	Barrister-at-law.
1833	J. P. Bartrum	American.
1833	George Musgrave	Curate of Marylebone.
1833	P. J. Ducarel	
1834	H. A. S. Atwood	Curate of Kenilworth.
1834	Henry F. Lyte	Perpetual Curate of Brixham.
1835	William Allen, D.D.	President of Bowdoin College.
1836	E. Farr	
1838	C. Foster and E. Colling	
1839	John Keble	Vicar of Hursley.

Date.	Name.	Rank or Occupation.
1840	George Burgess, D.D.	Bishop of Maine
1841	John Eden	Vicar of St. Nicholas', Bristol.
1843	Francis Skurray	Rector of Winterbourne, Dorset.
1844	E. Feilde	M.A., Pastor of Rock and Rennington.
1845	Thomas Spalding	Wholesale stationer.
1847	Joseph Irons	Calvinistic minister, Camberwell.
1847	B. T. H. Cole	Rector of Warbleton, Sussex.
1848	W. H. B.	
1850	Samuel McClure	American.
1850	Morris Williams	Clergyman of the Establishment.
1850	Frederick Fysh	Author of " Anastasis Examined."
1851	M. Montagu	Lieutenant in the Royal Navy.
1853	" A Layman "	
1854	Abner Jones	Professor of Music, New York.
1854	Edward Churton	Archdeacon of Cleveland.
1856	G. T. Townsend	Author of " Flowers from the Garden of the Church."
1857	Anonymous	
1858	Edgar A. Bowring	Member of Parliament for Exeter.
1859	" An Octogenarian "	
1859	Thomas Turner	Fellow of Trinity College, Cambridge.
1860	C. B. Cayley	Author of " Psyche's Interludes."
1862	W. C. Yonge	Minister at Henley-on-Thames.
1863	Arthur Malet	
1863	Robert Young	M.A., Minister of Free Church, Chapelton.
1863	William Milligan	Justice of the Peace.
1864	American Metrical Psalter	Bishops of the Episcopal Church.
1865	Viscount Massereene	10th Viscount Massereene and Ferrard.
1867	Dalman Hapstone	Master of Arts.
1868	James Keith	Bookseller at Dingwall, N.B.
1870	Thomas Slater	Author of " Compendium of Ancient History."
1871	John Burton	Timber-merchant.
1875	William Rees	Preacher, journalist, and poet.
1876	B. H. Kennedy, D.D.	Canon of Ely.
1877	Marquis of Lorne	Governor-general of Canada.
1878	D. C. McLaren, D.D.	American Doctor of Divinity.
1882	W. D. Seymour	Q.C., Recorder of Newcastle.
1883	" Ben-Tehillim "	
1883	David McLaren	Minister of Humbie.
1885	D. S. Wrangham	M.A., St. John's College, Oxford.

Although metrical versions of the Psalms were usually added to the Prayer-books, their use was never obligatory, if the Commonwealth Psalter be not excepted. No mention of them is made in the rubric. The anthem only is referred to : " In quires and places where they sing, here followeth the anthem." The rhymed Psalters were privileged, allowed, or permitted to be used, by royal or other authority. The following is a list of these privileged versions :—

Name.	Date.	Privilege or Permission.
Crowley . .	1549	Cum privilegio ad imprimendum solum.
Parker . .	1557?	Cum gratia et privilegio.
Sternhold . .	1562	Cum gratia et privilegio. Faithfully perused and allowed.
King James . .	1631-6	Allowed to be sung in all the churches, and authorized to be added to the Prayer-book.
Wither . .	1632	Authorized to be added to all editions of the Bible.
G. Sandys . .	1636	Cum privilegio Regiæ Majestatis.
Barton . .	1644	Printed by order of Parliament.
Rous . . .	1643-50	Ordered by both Houses of Parliament to be sung throughout the kingdom.
Tate and Brady .	1696	Allowed and permitted by royal authority to be used in all the churches.
Sir R. Blackmore	1721	Royal allowance that the same be permitted to be used in all the churches.

Dod is also stated to have received the royal sanction, but only one authority * has been found to verify the statement.

The writer has endeavoured, in the following

* J. H. Todd.

descriptions of the metrical Psalters, to supply the names of the authors who published their works anonymously or under fictitious names. In some cases he has been successful ; but five versions have baffled his research :—

ROBERT CROWLEY.

1549.—The Psalter of David, newely translated into Englysh Metre, in such sorte that it may the more decently, and wyth the more delyte of the mynde, be reade and songe of al men. Where-unto is added a note of four partes, wyth other thynges, as shall appeare in the Epistle to the Reader. Translated and Imprinted by Robert Crowley, in the yere of Our Lord MDXLIX, the xx day of September, and are to be solde in Eley rentes in Holbourne. Cum privilegio ad Imprimendum solum. BLACK LETTER.—*Brazenose College Library.* *

I. †

" That man is happy and blessed that hath not gone astraye
   In the counsel of wycked men, nor stand in synners waye.
   That man is blest, I say, that hath not sate in companye
   With scornful men that thyncke wysdom to rest in them
      onlye.
   But hath in the lawe of the Lorde set his onely delyht :
   And will in the same exercise hymselfe both daye and
      night."

XXIII.

" The Lorde is my Shepherde, and I shall never stand in
      nede ;
   For in pasture exceedinge good, He leadeth me to fede,

---

* The writer is indebted, for the extracts, to the courtesy of the Principal of Brazenose, the Rev. Albert Watson.

† Psalm i. The first verses of Psalm i. and Psalm xxiii. are given in all the versions.

He causeth me to laye me downe in pasture full of grasse ;
And dryveth me to caulme waters that be so cleare as
    glasse."

Crowley was a printer and bookseller in London,
who edited and published, among other works, the
" Visions of Pierce Plowman." During the reign of
Edward VI. he exercised the gift of preaching. He was
Fellow of Magdalene College, 1542 ; Prebendary of
St. Paul's, 1558 ; Rector of Cripplegate, where he was
buried.

MATTHEW PARKER.

1557 ?—The Whole Psalter translated into English Metre, which con-
    tayneth an hundreth and fifty Psalmes. By M. P. Imprinted
    at London by John Daye, dwelling over Aldersgate, beneath
    St. Martyn's. Cum gratia et privilegio. BLACK LETTER.—
    Brit. Mus. Lib.

I.

" An blest no doubt : who walketh not out,
    In wicked mens affayres ;
And strondth no daie : in sinners waie,
    Nor sitth in scorners chayres."

XXIII.

" The Lord so good : who geueth me food,
    My Shepheard is and guide :
How can I want : or suffer scant,
    When He defenth my side ?
To feede my neede : He will me leade
    To pastures greene and fat ;
He forth brought me : in libertie,
    To waters delicate."

Archbishop Parker, born 1504; Fellow of Corpus Christi, Oxford. Chaplain successively to Anne Boleyn, Henry VIII. (1537), and Edward VI.; Dean of Lincoln (1552), when deprived of his spiritualties by Queen Mary; and Archbishop of Canterbury from 1559 to his death in 1575. The Bishop's Bible was published under his direction in 1568.

Parker's version was probably printed in Holland, during his enforced retirement between 1533 and the accession of Queen Elizabeth. It must have been a work of considerable labour, and is undoubtedly one of the finest productions in black letter of the typographical art of the period. One of the copies—a few only of which were privately distributed—is in the British Museum. The Psalter is prefaced by a metrical address to the reader, and long translations from Athanasius, Basilius, Augustine, and Eusebius, on the use of the Psalms.

Each of the Psalms in Parker's Psalter is preceded by a collect, and followed by an argument or homily; and, at the end of the book, are added eight tunes, the "meane, contra, tenor, and base," separately written, with the following quaint description of the character of the music:—

> " 1. The first is meeke : devout to see,
>   2. The second sad : in maiestie,
>   3. The third doth rage : and roughly brayth,
>   4. The fourth doth frowne : and flattry playth,
>   5. The fifth delyth : and laugheth the more,
>   6. The sixth bewayleth : it weepeth full sore,
>   7. The seventh tredeth stoute : in forward race,
>   8. The eyghte goeth milde : in modest pace."

STERNHOLD AND HOPKINS.

1564.—The Whole Booke of Psalmes collected into English Meeter, by Thomas Sternhold, J. Hopkins, and others. Conferred with the Hebrew, with Apt Notes to sing them withal. Faithfully perused and allowed according to thorder appoynted in the Queens Maiestyes Injunction [51st Injunction Queen Elizabeth, 1559]. Very mete to be used of all sortes of people priuately for their godly solace and comfort, laying aparte all vngodly songes and balades, which tend only to the nourishing of vyce and corruption of youth. Imprinted at London by John Daye, dwelling over Aldersgate. Cum gratia et privilegio regiæ Maiestatis per septennium, 1564. —*Brit. Mus. Lib.*

I.

" The man is blest that hath not bent,
    to wicked rede his care,
Nor led his life as sinners do,
    nor sat in scorners chaire."

XXIII.

" My shepherd is the liuing Lord,
    nothing I therefore neede ;
In pastors fair with waters calm
    He set me for to fede.
He did conuert and glad my soule,
    and brought my mind in frame :
To walke in pathes of righteousnes
    for His most holy Name."

Thomas Sternhold died in 1549. In addition to his Psalms he also wrote, " Certain Chapters of the Proverbs of Solomon drawn into Metre."

The Sternhold version had the merit of being simple and popular ; yet Warton called it " the disgrace of sacred poetry;" and a later writer, who attempted its defence, concluded his argument by asserting that there was no proof that it did any harm: "that it ever *did* impede devotion has not even been attempted to be shown."

Of the 150 Psalms in this version, 40 were by Sternhold, 60 by Hopkins, 12 by Whittingham, 10 by Kethe, 1 by Pullain, and 26 by Norton.

GEORGE BUCHANAN.

1565 ?—* Psalmorvm Dauidis Paraphrasis Poetica, nunc primùm edita. Authore Georgio Buchanano, Scoto, pœtratrum nostri Sæculi facilè principe. Eiusdem Dauidis Psalmi aliquot à Th. B. V. Versi. Psalmi aliquot in versus itē Græcos nuper à diuersis translati. Apud Henricum Stephanum, & eius fratrem Robertū Stephanum, typographum Regium. Ex Privilegio Regis [impressum Parisiis, 1670].—*Brit. Mus. Lib.*

I.

"Felix ille animi, quem non de tramite recto,
Impia sacrilegæ flexit contagio turbæ:
Non iter erroris tenuit, sessorve cathedræ.
Pestiferæ, facilem dedit irrisoribus aurem."

XXIII.

"Tota quidè Domini terra est, et quicquid vbig.
Vel parca celat, vel benigna sufficit:
Quiq: colùt motésque feros càpósque feraces,
Verbèsque sanctes temperatus legibus." †

---

* This Latin version is inserted among the whole English metrical Psalters, because one author translated it into English, and others were evidently influenced by it.

† "Verbesque sanctis temporatas legibus" in Plantin Press copy, 1609.

George Buchanan, the Scotch historian, born 1506, died 1582, translated the Psalms into metrical Latin while confined in a monastery in Portugal, by the officers of the Inquisition. " His Latin translation of the Psalms shows him to have been a poet of a high order ; though he is, perhaps, more remarkable for the harmony of versification and richness of style than for strength of imagination." * Mackenzie says that he translated his Psalms "with such inimitable sweetness and elegancy that his version will be esteemed as long as the world endures, or men have any relish for poetry."

The accomplished author of the " History of Scotland " was appointed by the Assembly of the Scottish Nobility preceptor to the young prince, afterwards King James I., who found him a strict master, if we may rely on the story, too coarse for quotation, founded on the statement that the prince received from him once at least a severe whipping.

SIR PHILIP SIDNEY.

1580?—The Psalmes of David in Metre. By Sir Philip Sidney and his Sister, the Countess of Pembroke. Printed from the original MSS. in 1823 by the Chiswick Press.—*Brit. Mus. Lib.*

I.

" He blessed is who neither loosely treads
The straying steps as wicked councel leads,
    Ne for bad mates in way of sinners waiteth,
    Nor yet himself with idle scorners seateth."

* Thomas's " Dictionary of Biography."

XXIII.

" The Lord, the Lord my Shepheard is,
    And so can never I
        Tast missery.
He rests me in greene pasture his ;
    By waters still and sweete
        He guides my feete."

Sidney, nephew of Dudley, Earl of Leicester, soldier
and poet, whom the Prince of Orange judged to be
" one of the ripest and greatest councillors in Europe,"
was born in 1554, knighted in 1582, and slain in the
battle of Zutphen, 1586. His sister, the Countess
of Pembroke, also translated a play from the French
called "Antonius ; or, The Tragedy of Mark Anthony,
1575." She died in 1621. Her additions to the
Psalms do not reach the standard of her brother's.
The metre and the poetry, however, of either of these
Psalm-writers could never have become as popular
as the simpler although coarser rhymes of Sternhold
and Hopkins.

Ruskin, in the " Rock Honeycomb," says, " Nevertheless, I should not have thought it necessary to add
any other version of the Psalms to the accepted one
of the Prayer-book for use in St. George's Schools,
had not these paraphrases of Sir Philip contained
many illustrative or explanatory passages, making
the sense of the original more clear, while, at the
same time, their exquisitely accurate use of the
English language renders them, on the whole, the
best examples known for the early guidance of its
faithful students."

WILLIAM MYDDELTON.

1603.—Psalmæ y Brenhinol Brophwyd Dafydh, gwedi i cynghaneddu mewn mesurau Cymreic gann Capten Willm. Middelton, yn nesaf y gallodh at feddwl yr ysbryd glân. Simon Stafford. Thomas Salisbury ai printodh yn Llunden.—*Brit. Mus. Lib.*

The following extracts from the Psalms are taken from an edition, 1827, by Walter Davies :—

I.

" Gwynfyd o'i febyd gwinfaeth,
Gwirion dôn i'r gŵr nid aeth
Ar ol cyngor lwc anghall
Y drwg a ro 'i fryd ar wall ;
Ni saif yn ffordd brif-ffordd brys
Bechaduriaid, baich dyrys,
Nac ar gadair gyfair gawdd
Gwatwarwyr a gyd-dariawdd."

XXIII.

" Duw yw 'Mugail, arail un ;
Ni bydd (Duw a rydd da rym)
Arnaf, er a gaf o gam
Diau o'stad, eisiau dim.
Gwnaiff i'm orwedd, gyfedd goel,
Mewn porfa las, urddas wyl ;
A'm t'wysaw yn hylaw hael,
Ddifyr Iôr, wrth ddwfr arail."

Myddelton, who was educated at the university of Oxford, was a native of Gwenynog, Denbighshire ; served in the army under Elizabeth, afterwards had a command in a ship of war ; wrote a grammar, and

the "Art of Poetry," 1593. He was one of the three
captains who first publicly smoked tobacco in the
streets of London.

"His version is more skilful than useful. The
technical form is in accordance with the rules of
'assonance'—a well-known peculiarity of Welsh
poetry. For instance, taking the first lines above,
the following balancing of consonants will be ob-
served :—

> Gwynfyd | o'i febyd | gwinfaeth.
> *G   nf* | *g   nf*
> Gwirion dôn | i'r | gŵr nid aeth.
> *G r n d* | *g r n d*

In the fifth line another form of assonance is introduced—

> Ni saif yn ffordd brif-ffordd brys.

'Ffordd' and 'brif-ffordd' rhyme; and then the initial
consonants of the latter word are taken up again in
the last word of the line (*br . . . br*)" (Rev. H. Elvet
Lewis).

HENRY AINSWORTH.

1612.—The Booke of Psalmes Englished both in Prose and Metre. By
Henry Ainsworth. Amsterdam, printed by Thomas Staf-
ford, and are to be sold at his House at the signe of the
Flight of Brabant, upon the Milken-market, over against the
Deventer Wood-market. (Edit. 1644.)—*Brit. Mus. Lib.*

I.

" Blessed man, that doth not in the wickeds counsel walk :
Nor stand in synners way ; nor sit in seat of scornful-folk ;

But setteth in Iehovah's law, his pleasurefull delight,
And in his law doth meditate, by day and eke by night."

XXIII.

" Jehovah feedeth me, I shall not lack.
In grassy folds, He down dooth make me lye,
He gently leads me, quiet waters by."

Ainsworth was a leader among the Brownists in Amsterdam, where he died in 1622 or 1623. His annotations, showing immense study and labour, are massed in small type as a preface to the Psalms. His motive appears in his statement, "To the help, therefore, of the saints in the comfortable use of this exercise have I imployed my strength in this work ; and shall think it wel bestowed, if it may serve to God's glory and the good of His people."

Ainsworth was the author of a most learned commentary on the Five Books of Moses ; a master of Oriental languages and of Jewish antiquities. He was called the " rabbi of his age." [*]

HENRY DOD.

1620.—All the Psalmes of David, with certeine Songes and Canticles of Moses, Debora, Isaiah, Hezekiah, and others, not formerly extāt for song : and manie of the said Psalmes, dayly omitted, and not song at all, because of their defficult tunes. Now faithfully reduced into easie Meeter, fitting our common tunes. By H. D.—*Brit. Mus. Lib.*

---

[*] Neal's " History of the Puritans."

I.

"O blessed man that doth not in
　　The wickeds counsel walke :
Nor stand in sinners waye, nor sit
　　In seate of scornfull folke."

XXIII.

"The Lord my gracious Shepheard is,
　　So nothing want shall I ;
In pastures greene He makes me rest,
　　By th-sweete streames leading me."

In an address to the Christian reader the author
states that he had, in 1603, translated nine of the
Psalms for the use of his family. They were so well
received by his friends that he had them printed, and
it pleased "our dread soveraigne" to privilege the
same ; and then he was requested to versify the
whole in simple metre, which he did, and after wait-
ing nearly eighteen years for "some godly learned,"
whom he hoped might have done it better, he finally
printed it.

EDMUND PRYS.

1621.—Llyfr y Psalmau, wedi ei Cyfieihv, a'i Cyfansoddi ar fesvr
　　cerdd yn Gymraeg. Drwy waith Edmwnd Prys, Archdiacon
　　Meirionydd. A'i Printio yn Llundain.

I.

"Sawl in rodia, dedwydd yw
　　yn ol drwg ystryw gyngor,
Ni saif ar ffordd troseddwyr ffol,
　　nid eiste 'n 'stol y gwatwor."

XXIII.

" Yr Arglwydd yw fy Mugail clau,
      ni âd byth eisiau arnaf ;
  Mi a gâf orwedd mewn porfa fras
      ar lan dwfr gloywlas araf.
  Fe goledd f'enaid, ac a'm dwg
      'rhyd llwybrau diddrwg cyfion ;
  Er mwyn ei enw mawr dilys.
      Fo'm tywys ar yr union."

Edmund Prys was Archdeacon of Merioneth, born
at Harlech about 1541, and died 1624. He was
educated at St. John's College, Cambridge, appointed
archdeacon in 1576, and a Canon of St. Asaph, 1602.
A man of scholarly attainments, he had an intimate
knowledge of Hebrew, and was an eminent poet
among his people. A great number of his compositions have been preserved, mostly in manuscript.

" In the verse quoted above from his version of
Ps. xxiii. one characteristically Celtic touch deserves
to be noticed. The Celtic imagination delights in
nature-colours. So we have the ' still waters ' of the
Hebrew bard minutely described as the ' clear blue
water slow ' " (Rev. H. Elvet Lewis).

KING JAMES I.

1631.—The Psalmes of King David translated by King James.   Pictorial title-page representing King David on one side and King James on the other, holding up this new version upon which the Holy Spirit is descending.   Facing the picture: "Chas. R.   Haveing caused this translation of the Psalmes (whereof oure late deare father was author) to be perused, and it being found to be exactly and truely done, we doe hereby authorise the same to be Imprinted according to the Patent graunted thereupon, and doe allow them to be sung in all the Churches of our Dominion, recommending them to all our good subjects for that effect."   Oxford, printed by William Turner, printer to the famous University.—*Brit. Mus. Lib.*

I.

"The man is blest that doth not walke
Where wicked Counsells guide;
Nor in the way of sinners stands,
Nor scorners sits beside."

XXIII.

"The Lord of all my Shepheard is,
I shall from want be free:
He makes me in greene pastures lie,
And near calm streams to be."

This version is in reality that of William Alexander, afterwards Sir William Alexander (Earl of Stirling), who was the author of several dramas.   Jacob, in his "Lives and Characters of the Poets," "to shew that this nobleman sometimes wrote in a very good strain," quoted the following lines :—

"Love is a Joy, which upon Pain depends;
A drop of Sweet drown'd in a Sea of Sowres.

What folly does begin, that Fury ends ;
They hate for Ever, who have lov'd for Hours."

Another King James's version, apparently by other authors, although Lord Stirling's consent was required for the alterations, appeared in

1636.—The Psalms of David, translated by King James. London, printed for Thomas Harper. BLACK LETTER.—*Brit. Mus. Lib.*

I.

" The man is blest, who to walke in th' ungodlies counsell
   hates,
   And stands not in the sinners way, nor sits in scorners
   seats."

XXIII.

" The Lord of all, my Shepheard is, I shall from want be
   free :
   He makes me in green pastures lye, and neare calm
   streams to be."

Through the Civil War and its results, Sir William Alexander lost any pecuniary benefit he might have anticipated from the patent for sole printing which the king gave him ; but the "trustie and well-beloved coadjutor" of King James had been consoled by a peerage. As "Lord of Stirling," he enjoyed the reward of his silence concerning the little share his royal master had in the King James version of 1631. Stirling was born in 1580.

GEORGE WITHER.

1632.—The Psalmes of David, translated into Lyrick-Verse, according to the scope of the Original, and Illustrated with a Short Argument, and a Briefe Prayer, or Meditation ; before and after every Psalme. By George Wither. Imprinted in the Neatherlands, by Cornelis Gerrits Van Breughel. Dedicated to the Princess Elizabeth, Queen of Bohemia. (Reprint published by the Spencer Society.)—*Brit. Mus. Lib.*

I.

" Blest is he who neither straies
　　Where the Godless man misguideth,
Neither stands in sinners waies,
　　Nor in scorners chair abideth."

XXIII.

" The Lord my Pastor daignes to be,
　　I nothing, now, shall need ;
To drinck sweet springs He bringeth mee,
　　And on green meads to feed."

George Wither was one of Oliver Cromwell's major-generals, and held the command of the county of Surrey. After the Restoration, he was long a prisoner in Newgate and the Tower. Born in 1588, he died on the 2nd of May, 1667, aged seventy-eight. In 1619, he published a Preparation to the Psalter, and was concerned in succeeding years in what may be called the Battle of the Psalters, and much other controversy. Wither tried to supersede the use of the Sternhold and Hopkins version by his own, and succeeded in getting a patent from the king, one of the stipulations of which directed that his version should be added to all copies of the Bible.

He entered into competition with the contemporary versions of Rous and Barton when the Assembly of Divines at Westminster consulted about a new Psalter; but Rous held the field with the Presbyterians and others in England, Scotland, and America, the Sternhold and Hopkins version retaining its sole authority in the churches of the Establishment.

Wither's office of major-general was not bestowed upon him on account of any military education. He was a lawyer, and was taunted by his opponents with the fact when he was advocating the claims of his new Psalter ; being accused of " indecently obtruding upon the divine calling." He replied, indignantly, "I wonder what divine calling Hopkins and Sternhold had more than I have, that their metrical Psalms may be allowed of, rather than my hymns. Surely, if to have been *groome of the privie chamber* were sufficient to qualify them, that profession which I am of, may as well fit me for what I have undertaken."

GEORGE SANDYS.

1636.—A Paraphrase upon the Psalmes of David, set to new Tunes for private devotion, and a thorough Base for Voice or Instrument, by Henry Lawes, one of the gentlemen of His Majesties Chappell Royall. By George Sandys. Dedicated to the Best of Men and most excellent of Princes, Charles ; by the Grace of God King of Great Britaine, France, and Ireland ; Lord of the Foure Seas ; of Virginia ; the Vast Territories adjoyning ; and dispersed Islands of the Western Ocean, by the humblest of his Servants. Printed in the Yeare 1648.— *Brit. Mus. Lib.*

I.

"That man is truly blest who never strays
   By false advice, nor walkes in sinners wayes,
   Nor sits infected with their scornful pride,
   Who God contemne, and Pietie deride."

XXIII.

"The Lord my Shepheard, me His sheepe
   Will from consuming Famine keepe,
   He fosters me in fragrant meads,
   By softly sliding waters leads."

The copy of the 1636 edition in the British Museum Library is entitled—

A Paraphrase vpon the Psalmes of David, and vpon the Hymnes dispersed throughout the Old and New Testaments. By G. S. London : At the Bell, in St. Pauls Church Yard, CIƆ.IƆC.XXXVI. Cum Privilegio Regiæ Majestatis.

And there is added the following : "Summa Approbationis. Perlegi hoc Poema Paraphrasticum in Psalmos Davidis, et alios Hymnos Sacros, in quo nihil reperio S. Paginæ contrarium, quo minus cum utilitate, ut et summa lectorum voluptate imprimatur. Dat ex Ædibus Lambethanis, Novemb. 28. 1635. Guil. Bray, R^mo. P. D. A. Cant. Capellan Domesticus."

This version also contains a metrical address from Lord Falkland, who says of his "noble friend, George Sandys"—

> "Yet now thou hast
> Diverted to a Purer Path thy Quill;
> And chang'd Parnassus Mount to Sions Hill:
> So that blest David might almost Desire
> To heare his Harp thus echo'd by thy Lyre."

Sandys was born in 1577, at Bishopsthorpe, the palace of his father, the Archbishop of York. He was a Gentleman of the Privy Chamber to Charles I. During his extensive travels he occupied for a time the post of Treasurer of the English colony of Virginia, in America, where he translated a "Metamorphis" of Ovid. At a later period he wrote "Christ's Passion; a Tragedy," and rhymed some of the books of the Old Testament.

Richard Baxter, describing a visit he made to the seat of Sandys' nephew, Mr. Wyatt, at Boxley Abbey, where the poet died in 1643, said it did him good to see upon an old stone wall in the summer-house, "In that place Mr. G. Sandys, after his Travels over the world, retired himself for his poetry and contemplations."

ROTTERDAM VERSION.

1638.—The Booke of Psalmes in English· Meeter.　Printed for Henry Tutill, Bookseller, at Rotterdam.—*Lambeth Library.*

I.

"'The man is blessed that to walke
　In wicked wayes doth feare,
And stands not in the sinners path
　Nor sits in scorners chaire."

XXIII.

" My shepheard is the living Lord
　And He that doth me feed ;
How can I then lacke any thing
　Whereof I stand in need?
In pastures greene and flourishing,
　He makes me down to lye,
And after drives me to the streames
　Which run most pleasantly."

Apparently the author was a Puritan divine. He says, " Apprehending for many years past that a Forme wholly new would not please many, who are fastned to things usuall and accustomed, I assaied onely to change some pieces of the usuall version, even such as seemed to call aloud, and as it were undeniably for a Change. These being seene, it was desired that they should be increased ; which being done, they are here subjoyned."

RICHARD BRATHWAITE, OR RICHARD BURNABY.

1633.—The Psalmes of David, the King and Prophet, and of other Holy Prophets, paraphras'd in English. Conferred with the Hebrew VERITIE, set forth by *B. Arias Montanus*, together with the Latine, Greek Septuagint, and Chaldee Paraphrase. By R. B. London, printed by Robert Young, for Francis Constable, and are to be sold at his Shop under St. Martin's Church neere Ludgate.—*Brit. Mus. Lib.*

I.

" Blest is the man, whose walks are cleer
 From wicked counsells aire ;
To sinners way who stands not neer,
 Nor sits in scorners chaire."

XXIII.

" My shepheard is the Lord, whose care
 Provides me fold and food :
Whose goodness, plenteous and to spare,
 Supplies my want of good.
In pastures green He makes mee lye,
 And softly lodge my side ;
He leads mee forth where pleasantly
 The streames of stillness glide."

Richard Brathwaite—born 1588, died 1673—a voluminous writer, was at one time Deputy-Lieutenant of the county of Westmoreland. His works were chiefly in rhyme.

Luke Milbourne, in the preface to his own Psalms, alludes to the R. B. version as Mr. Burnaby's book. This allusion, and another in an old copy of Milbourne in his

G

possession, where there is a manuscript note to the same effect, strongly convinces Mr. Taylor, of Peter-head, that the R. B. Psalm-book is by Burnaby, not Brathwaite. Mr. Holland was of a similar opinion. But Mr. Hazlewood, editor of "Barnabee's Journal," which he discovered to be by Richard Brathwaite, is confident that the Psalms are by the same author. The Rev. Thomas Corser, editor of "Collectanea Anglo Poetica," holds the same view.

THE BAY PSALM-BOOK.

1640.—The Whole Book of Psalmes Faithfully translated into English Metre. Whereunto is prefixed a discourse declaring not only the lawfulness, but also the necessity of the heavenly ordinance of singing Scripture Psalmes in the Churches of God. Imprinted 1640.—*From Reprint in Brit. Mus. Lib.*

I.

"O Blessed man, that in th-advice
   of wicked men doth walk :
Nor stands in sinners way, nor sit
   in chayre of sinful folk."

XXIII.

"The Lord to mee a Shepheard is,
   want therefore shall not I,
He in the folds of tender grasse
   doth cause me downe to lie."

This book was the first printed in North America. It was versified under the supervision of the Rev. Richard Mather of Dorchester, the Rev. Thomas Weld, and the Rev. John Eliot of Roxbury; and was published at Cambridge, New England, by Mr. Stephen Daye.

The preface states, " If therefore the verses are not alwayes so smooth and elegant as some may desire and expect, let them consider that God's Altar needs not our pollishings : Ex. 20 ; for wee have respected rather a plaine translation, than to smooth our verses with the sweetnes of any paraphrase."

An English edition was printed in 1647, a copy of which is in the British Museum Library ; and in ten years the Bay Psalm-book passed through twenty-seven editions.

Mr. Shepherd, of Cambridge, Mass., noting the " different genius " of the writers of Roxbury and Dorchester, addressed them—

> " You Roxbury poets, keep clear of the crime
> Of missing to give us very good rhyme.
> And you of Dorchester, your verses strengthen,
> And with the text's own word you will them lengthen."

The Bodleian Library possesses a copy of this very rare book. James Lenox, founder of the Lenox Library, New York, hunted among old black-letter books in England for seven years before his persistence was rewarded by finding the invaluable volume in a bundle of black-letter Psalm-books, knocked down to him at a book sale in London for nineteen shillings. He afterwards bought a complete library for £2000, chiefly to obtain another Bay Psalm-book. This second copy was subsequently sold for £250.

FRANCIS ROUS.

1643.*—The Psalmes of David in English Meeter, set forth by Francis
Rous. It is this day ordered (April 17, 1643) by the Com-
mittee of the House of Commons in Parliament, that the Book entitled *The Psalmes of David*, etc. (according
to desires of many reverend Ministers), be published for the
generall use : And for the true correcting of it, be printed
by these the Author shall approve. (Signed) John White.
I do appoint Philip Nevill and Peter Whaley to print these
Psalmes. (Signed) Francis Rous. London, printed by
James Young, for Philip Nevill, at the signe of the Gun in
Ivie Lane.—*Brit. Mus. Lib.*

I.

" The man is blessed that to walk
    In wicked waies doth feare,
And stands not in the sinners path,
    Nor sits in scorners chaire."

XXIII.

" My shepheard is the living Lord,
    And He that doth me feed ;
How can I then lack any thing
    Whereof I stand in need ? "

Another edition appeared in

1646.—The Psalmes of David in English Meeter. London, printed by
Miles Flesher, for the Company of Stationers. Die Veneris
4 [14] Novemb. 1645. It is this day ordered by the Commons
assembled in Parliament, That this Book of Psalmes set forth
by Mr. Rous, and perused by the Assembly of Divines, be
forthwith printed : And that it be referred to Mr. Rous to take
care for the printing thereof : and that none do presume to
print it, but such as shall be authorised by him. H. Elsinge,
Cler. Parl. Dom. Com.—*Brit. Mus. Lib.*

---

* Cotton gives the date 1641 as that of the first edition.

It was succeeded in the following year by an edition which had been revised by the author, who had made considerable alterations.

1647.—The Whole Book of Psalmes. Faithfully translated to English Metre. By Francis Rous.—*Brit. Mus. Lib.*

I.

" O Blessed Man, that in th'advice
Of wicked doth not walk.
Nor stand in sinners way, nor sit
In chair of scornfull folk."

XXIII.

" The Lord to me a shepheard is,
Want therefore shall not I ;
He in the folds of tender grasse
Doth cause me down to lie."

" Our old friend Rouse," as Carlyle calls him, was a younger son of Sir Anthony Rous, and was born at Halton, in Cornwall, in 1579. He was M.P. for Truro in the Long Parliament ; at first Chairman, and then Speaker for a month of the Barebones Parliament ; successively a member of Cromwell's Council and his House of Lords ; and a lay member of the Westminster Assembly of Divines. During the Commonwealth he was Provost of Eton. The origin of the derisive title, " Illiterate Jew of Eton," was doubtless in reference to Rous's proposition to form the English Commonwealth after the model of the Jewish theocracy. He " looked upon Cromwell as a compound of the characters of Moses and Joshua." How little the term "illiterate" was deserved is seen by his antecedents. He took a B.A. degree at Oxford, afterwards studied law, and then, it is said, took orders and preached. He was "principal trier and approver of preachers." In 1650 he published a thick octavo, "Mella Patrum," containing, says Chalmers, "the beauties of the Fathers of the first three centuries." His writings were collected in a folio printed in 1657, under the title of "The Works of Francis Rous, esq.; or, Treatises and Meditations dedicated to the Saints, and to the Excellent throughout the three nations."

Rous died in 1658. He was buried with great pomp at Eton, and a standard pennon, and other things relating to a baron, were erected over his grave; but these were taken away at the Restoration. His portrait is still preserved in the Provost's Lodge at Eton.

In the preface Rous states, "As for other objections taken from the difficulty of Ainsworth's tunes, and the corruptions in our common Psalm-Books, we hope they are answered in the new edition of the Psalmes, which we here present to God and His people."

WILLIAM BARTON.

1644.—The Book of Psalms in Metre, lately translated with Many Whole Ones, and choice Collections of the Old Psalms added to the First Impression. Printed by Order of Parliament, and now much Augmented and Amended with the cream and flower of the Best Authors, all following the common Tunes at this day used in and about London ; with the approbation of more than fourty eminent Divines of the City and most of them of the Assembly. By William Barton, Mr. of Arts, and Minister of John Zecharies, London. Printed by G. M. and are to be sold by S. Gelibrand, at the Brazen Serpent, in P. Church Yard, T. Kirton next Goldsmith's Hall in Foster Lane, T. Underhill at the Bible in Wood Street, and Stephen Bowled at the signe of the Bible in Pope's Head Alley. (Edit. 1645.) —*Brit. Mus. Lib.*

I.

" The man is blest that neither strays
　　By counsels of ungodly men,
Nor standeth in the sinner's way,
　　Nor sits in scorners seat with them."

XXIII.

" My Lord's my Shepherd to provide,
I shall be sure to be supply'd,
　　And by this means
In pastures green I couch between
　　The silent streams."

Barton's Psalter has a dedication in rhyme to Sir John Wollaston, knight and alderman, and a number of poetical testimonials from friends complimenting his translations as " sweet," " exact," " apt," " excellent," " exquisite," and " elaborate." They take the place, apparently, of the modern practice of extracting

favourable notices of the press. Alernative versions of
a number of stanzas and lines are added at the end of
the book, " that the judgment of the intelligent reader
may mend the rest (if any change be needful) by his
own skill."

Like King James's versions, those of Barton dis-
played an amount of revision that deserved to be
called "re-writing." These are the verses of the 1644
edition in Mr. Taylor's collection :—

I.

" That man is blest and blest agen
    That doth not walk astray,
By counsels of ungodly men,
    Nor stands in sinners way."

XXIII.

" The Lords my Shepherd to provide
    No wofull want shall I abide :
In pastures best he makes me rest,
    He leads me by still waters side."

Barton took his degree of B.A. at Oxford in
1633, and in 1656 was Minister of St. Martin's,
Leicester. The living of Cadeby was given to him
by Cromwell, and he was one of the ejected ministers
in 1662. His son says that he caused his new translation of the Psalms to be published in 1644 ; the impression being speedily exhausted. Another edition
appeared in 1645, and a third in 1654. Within a
short time after Barton revised his last work for the
press, " he sickened, and upon the 14 day of May,
1678, it pleased God to call him out of this life to His

heavenly Kingdom, being aged about 74 or 75." His amended edition, "as he left it finished in his life-time," was printed in 1682, and continued to be re-printed until 1705. He also published " Six Centuries of Hymns," reprinted in 1688.

ZACHARY BOYD.

1648.—The Psalmes of David in Meeter : with the Prose interlined. By Mr. Zachary Boyd, Preacher of God's Word. Dedicated to the Right Reverend the faithfull Ministers of God's Word, of Britain and Ireland. Printed at Glasgow by the Heires of George Anderson.—*Brit. Mus. Lib.*

I.

" Blest is the man who walks not in
    Th'ungodlies counsell ill,
Nor stands in sinners way, nor doth
    In scorners seat sit still."

XXIII.

" The Lord's my Shepherd, I'le not want,
    He makes me down to ly
In pastures green, and He me doth
    Lead the still waters by."

Boyd was Minister of the Barony Church, Glasgow, and Lord Rector of the University of Glasgow, 1634, 1635, and 1645. Died 1653, aged about sixty-five. He left behind him seventeen quarto manuscript volumes, among which were the Four Evangels, and many incidents of Holy Writ in rhyme. " He put his hand to the work of the Psalms at the direction of

the General Assembly at Edinburgh, anno 1644"
(Preface).

Boyd was the author of "Zion's Flowers; or,
Christian Poems for Spiritual Edification," commonly
called "Boyd's Bible;" also "Last Battell of the
Soule in Death" (1628).

THE SCOTCH PSALTER.

1650.—Psalms of David in Meeter, newly translated and dilligently
compared with the Originall Text, and former translations,
more plain and smooth and agreeable to the Text than any
heretofore. Allowed by the Authority of the Generall
Assembly of the Kirk of Scotland, and appointed to be sung
in Congregations and Families. Edinburgh, printed by
Evan Tyler.—*Brit. Mus. Lib.*

I.

"That man hath perfect blessednesse
Who walketh not astray
In counsell of ungodly men,
Nor stand in sinners way,
Nor sitteth in the scorners chaire."

XXIII.

"The Lord's my Shepheard, I'le not want,
He makes me down to ly
In pastures green; He leadeth me
The quiet waters by."

This Psalter was a revised version of the Rous
edition, authorized by the Westminster Assembly, as
will be seen by the following appointment: "Edin-

burgh, 23d November, 1649. The Commissioners of
the General Assembly having with great diligence
considered the Paraphrase of the Psalmes in Meeter,
sent from the Assembly of Divines in England by
our Commissioners while they were there . . . do
appoint them to be printed and published for public
use after the first day of May, 1650."

THE NEW ENGLAND PSALM-BOOK.

1650.—The Psalms, Hymns, and Spiritual Songs of the Old and New
Testament, faithfully translated into English Meeter, for the
Edification and Comfort of the Saints, in publick and Private,
especially in New England. London, printed for Richard
Chiswell, at the Rose and Crown, in St. Paul's Church
Yard. [English edit. 1680.]—*Brit. Mus. Lib.*

I.

" O Blessed Man, that walks not in
Th'advice of wicked men,
Nor standeth in the sinners way,
Nor scorners seat sits in."

XXIII.

" The Lord to me a Shepheard is,
Want therefore shall not I ;
He in the folds of tender-grass
Doth make me down to lye."

Like the Scotch Psalter, the New England Psalm-
book is largely a revised Rous version. In 1647
President Dunster, of Harvard College, assisted by
Mr. Richard Lyon and thirty other learned and pious

persons, attempted a better version than the Bay
Psalm-book. After three years' labour the new Psalter
was completed, and came into general use in America.
A copy of the twenty-fourth edition, printed at Boston,
New England, 1737, is in the Library of the British
Museum. It was also sung in many English congre-
gations until as late as 1717. " It went through fifty
editions, including those published in Europe." *

HENRY KING, D.D.

1651.—The Psalmes of David, from the New Translation of the Bible,
turned into Meeter. To be sung after the Old Tunes used
in the Churches. London, printed by Ed. Griffin, and are
to be sold by Humphrey Moseley, at the Prince's Arms in
St. Paul's Church Yard. Ian. the 7th, 1650. Imprimatur
John Downaine. Allowed of the Company of Stationers.
—*Dr. Williams's Library.*

I.

" The man is blest whose feet not tread,
    By wicked counsailes led :
Nor stands in that perverted way,
    In which the sinners stray ;
Nor joynes himself unto the chaire
    Where scorners seated are."

XXIII.

" The Lord my Shepheard is, and guide ;
    I shall no want abide ;
He makes me lye in fruitfull meads,
    And by stil waters leads."

* Thomas's "History of Printing in America."

Bishop King, born in 1591, was Chaplain to James I., Residentiary of St. Paul's, and Canon of Christ Church. He took his doctor's degree in 1625, and held the see of Chichester from 1641 till his death in 1669.

The author says, in his introduction, " The generall distast taken at some unhandsome expressions in the Old [versions] which bothe disfigured the meaning of the Holy Ghost, and reproached our English Tongue (that did not afford a decent cloathing to preserve them from the scorne of those who apprehended any occasion to quarrell us), invited me to try in some Few, whither they might not in the plainest dress of language be freed from those disparagements of the Text which gave offence. After I had privately shewed Those (intended no farther than for an assay) persuasion of Friends, who had power to command, made me (having now leisure from those greater employments, to which I was called more than I ever expected) willing to run through the rest."

He trusts that his attempt will be acceptable to " the Most Renowned Mother Church of England."

JOHN WHITE.

1655.—David's Psalms in Metre, agreeable to the Hebrew, to be sung in usual Tvnes, to the benefit of the Churches of Christ. By the Reverend Mr. John White, Minister of God's Word in Dorchester. London, printed by S. Griffin for J. Rothwel, at the Fountain and Bear in Goldsmith's Row in Cheapside. —*Brit. Mus. Lib.*

I.

"Thrice blessed is he, that to walk
In ill-mens counsel fears ;
Nor stands in sinners way, nor sits
At rest in scorners chairs."

XXIII.

"My shepheard is the living Lord,
And He that doth me feed ;
I cannot then want anything
Whereof I stand in need."

John White, called the "Patriarch of Dorchester," had been the rector there for forty-two years. He was one of the clerical assessors of the Assembly of Divines at Westminster, in 1643. Born 1574, and died 1648. His version was not published until after his death, as he did not wish to enter into competition with other versionists, who were "strugling which of them should get the Civil sanction."

The preface was written by Stanley Gower, who writes thus of White's Psalms : "Thus to sing them in good meeter, and easie Tunes, shall find Vulgar quantities and Smooth Verse, without harsh synalæphas, as in some other versions. No New Version, *For he saith the old is better*, hath not well drank of either; for the old prose needeth not more New Translation, then in many places doth the old Meeter."

SAMUEL WOODFORD, D.D.

1667.—A Paraphrase upon the Psalmes of David and the Canticles, with
Select Hymns of the Old and New Testament, to which is
added occasional Compositions in Verse. By Samuel Wood-
ford, D.D. Printed and sold by Samuel Keble, at the Turk's
Head in Fleet Street. (1713. Reprint of the edit. of 1678.)
—*Brit. Mus. Lib.*

The title of the 1667 edition was—

A Paraphrase upon the Psalms of David. By Sam. Woodford.
London. Printed by R. White for Octavian Pullen, neer the
Pump, in Little Brittan.

I.

" Thrice happy Man, who in the gloomy ways
Of careless Sinners, never blindly strays,
In Counsel stands not to maintain their part,
Nor boldly thrusts into the Chair
His own to vent, or others scoffs to hear."

XXIII.

" The Mighty God, who all things do's sustain
That God, who nothing made in vain,
Who nothing that He made did e're disdain
The Mighty God my Shepherd is,
He is my Shepherd, I His sheep."

Ps. i., in the 1667 edition, reads thus—

" Thrice happy man, who in the beaten wayes
Of Careless sinners never blindly strayes
In their assemblies, nor maintains their part,

Their scoffs, or their debates will hear,
But leaves the place as well as chair
And keeps his ears as guiltless as his heart."

Woodford was born in 1636, died in 1700. He was a voluminous writer, and at one time proposed to versify the first chapter of the Book of Genesis, as a "History of the First Great Week of the World," in which he promised himself great assistance from the Royal Society. After his principal rhyming works were published, Woodford entered into holy orders, took the degree of B.D., and was Rector of Hartley Malduith, Hants, and Prebendary of Winchester.

"After versifying the civ. Psalm," he writes, " I know not how, on a suddain, all my heart was laid, and the greatness of the labour, together with my own insufficiency, deterred me at the time from proceeding any further. Hereupon for about three years the design slept with me, till, reading over with a little more than ordinary intention the cxiv. Psalm of Mr. Cowley's, I was again warm'd, and in imitation of him I was resolved once more to try how well or ill I could write after so excellent a copy."

Anthony Wood describes Woodford as " a violist."

SIR JOHN DENHAM.

1668 ?—A Version of the Psalms of David Fitted to the Tunes used in
Churches. By the Honourable Sir John Denham, Knight
of the Bath. London, printed for J. Bowyer, at the Rose in
Ludgate Street. (Edit. 1714.)—*Brit. Mus. Lib.*

I.

" Blest is the man, who never treads
   Those paths, where evil Counsel leads ;
   In sin's deep Ways, nor standing fast,
   Nor on high Seats, with Scorners plac'd."

XXIII.

" My Shepherd is the living Lord ;
   To me my Food and Ease
   The rich luxuriant Fields afford ;
   The Streams my Thirst appease."

Sir John was the author of " Cooper's Hill " and other poems.   He was born in 1615, died in 1668, and was buried in Westminster Abbey.

There are two prefaces—one by Heighes Woodford, and another by the author, who says, " I consulted the best commentators, and three paraphrasists—Buchanan, Woodford,* and Sandys."

" He consecrated his poetical powers to religion, and made a metrical version of the Psalmes of David.   In this attempt he has failed : but in sacred poetry who has succeeded ? " (Dr. Johnson).

" Denham and Waller improved our versification, and Dryden perfected it " (Prior).

---

* Denham either wrote his Psalms in the last year of his life, or he must have had access to Woodford's manuscript, which was transcribed at Albrook, in 1665.

H

MILES SMYTH.

1668.—The Psalms of King David Paraphrased, and turned into English Verse, according to the Common Metre, as they are usually sung in Parish Churches. By Miles Smyth. London, printed for T. Garthwait—in S. Bartholomews Hospital, near Smithfield.—*Brit. Mus. Lib.*

I.

"Blest is the man who walks not where
 Ungodly Counsels guide ;
Nor stands in sinful ways ; nor sits
 With those who God deride."

XXIII.

"The Lord's my Shepherd, Therefore I
 Can nothing want ; In flow'ry meads
And Pastures green He makes me lie,
 And to the quiet Waters leads."

In the first edition, 1664, the twenty-third Psalm reads—

"God, by whose Providence we live,
 Whose care secures our rest,
My shepherd is, no ill can touch
 Nor want my Soul infest.

"He makes Luxuriant flow'ry Meads
 Serve me for Food and Ease ;
And leads me where the cooling Streams,
 My thirsty heat appease."

Smyth was secretary to Dr. Sheldon, Archbishop of Canterbury. "The author of this version of the Psalms of King David, considering the Excellency, not only of the Divine matter they contain, but of the Sacred Rapture wherein they were penned, and the sublime Poetry wherewith they were set out, and adorned by the Royal and Inspired Prophet, could not but blush to think, how that Metre in which our Parochial Churches usually sing them, hath disguised so Eminent a part of the Holy Writ, which bears a more than ordinary stamp of that ever-blessed Spirit by which it was dictated and given. This gave the Author occasion to make Essay, whether (without taking the advantages of an unconfined Fancy) it might not be easie enough (even in that narrow and low kind of Verse) to make them speak their own genuine sense, in proper and smooth English" (Preface).

FRANCIS ROBERTS, D.D.

1674.—The Book of Hymnes or Praises, viz. the Book of Psalmes, translated immediately out of the Hebrew, and Analytically Expounded. Together with a General Preface, prefixed to the Whole Book of Psalmes. By F. R., D.D. London, Printed by J. R., and are to be sold by Peter Parker, at his Shop at the Leg and Star over against the Royal Exchange, and Thomas Guy, at the Corner-shop of Little Lumbard Street and Cornhill. 1674 [published in folio, with Dr. Roberts's " Clavis Bibliorum "].—*Brit. Mus. Lib.*

I.

" The-Blessednesses of that-man,
    That hath not walkt astray
In Counsel of the wicked men,
    Nor stood in sinners way,
Nor hath in seat of scorners sate."

XXIII.

"I shall not lack : the Lord *a* me feeds,
He-makes-me-down-to-lie *
In folds of budding grass : me leads
Of rests the waters by."

"To this end the grand and primary intendment in this Version hath been, to bring it to the greatest nearness possible unto the Hebrew, that as much of God, and as little of man, as may be might appear therein, and the spirit of God's people might consequently receive the more abundant satisfaction and consolation in this sacred PSALM melody" (Preface).

Dr. Roberts, "Pastor of Austin's," was assistant to the Commissioners appointed by Parliament for the ejection of scandalous ministers and schoolmasters, and one of the Presbyterian divines who protested against the sentence passed upon Charles I. by Parliament. He died in 1675.

Another edition appeared in that year.

1675.—Clavis Bibliorum. The Key of the Bible, unlocking the richest Treasury of the Holy Scriptures, etc. Whereunto are added the Metrical Version of the Whole Book of Psalmes, Immediately out of the Hebrew : And the Analytical Exposition of every Psalm. Fourth edition, diligently revised. By Francis Roberts.

"The meetre of this version," says the preface, "is so ordered that Barbarismes, Obsolete and antiquated Expressions, and light frothy Poetical flashes are studiously therein declined."

* The hyphens used explain the terms "implicitly comprised under the force and emphasis of the Hebrew word, and linked thereto with a makkaph (-)" (Preface).

Dr. Roberts's verses are in simple long and common metres ; before each Psalm is a summary of contents ; and after each "the Kinde, Penman, and Occasion, the Scope, and the Analysis of the Principal parts."

RICHARD GOODRIDGE.

1684.—The Psalter or Psalms of David Paraphras'd in Verse. Set to new Tunes, and so designed that by Two Tunes onely, the whole Number of Psalms (Four onely excepted) may be sung ; one of which Tunes is already known (being the usual Tune of the C. Psalm), the other Tunes onely are New ; but any one of them being learnt, all the other Psalms may be sung by that one onely Tune : As on the contrary any one Psalm may be sung by all the new Tunes. So that a greater facility for those who are less able to sing, or a greater variety for those who are more able, cannot reasonably be desired or afforded. The Second Edition, wherein the whole Number is Compleated. By Richard Goodridge. Oxford, printed by J. Lichfield, Printer to the University. For Jo. Crosley.—*Chichester Cathedral Library.* *

I.

" Blessings croun his fair Soul, who does not stray,
  Led by false Counsels, in the Sinners way :
  Who has not sate in the Proud Scorners Seat,
  Who mock at Piety, and God forget.
  That in Gods Law hath plac'd his whole delight,
  And makes the Law his study Day and Night."

XXIII.

" How can I want, whose Shepherd is my God ?
  His mighty Scepter deigns to be a Rod ;

* The author is indebted to Sir R. G. Raper for the extracts from this scarce version.

Calm Streams, cool Shades, my high Refreshments be,
My Soul has Heavens own rest, Tranquillity."

Preface : " What offence is generally taken, and how justly, at our English Version of Davids Psalms into Meeter, is sufficiently known. Some have endeavoured to make it more tolerable by expunging those many low and indecent Expressions, and putting others in their Places : but the attempt is fruitless. Wherefore, a New Version is doubtless the only Expedient. All should humbly present the utmost they are able to contribute towards the copying out the Beauty of the Divine Original. The Reader I hope will believe that I present them out of Duty, and so excite those of greater Abilities to pursue it by a joynt Endeavour. I have endeavour'd to avoid all obscurity, that it should be intelligible to all, High and Low, Rich and Poor. In order to which I have not rendred it litterally, but by way of Paraphrase. In the choice of words and expressions, I have taken care to use such as may be intelligible to the meanest. It seems expedient that (as the Original it self has given the Example) Paraphrase should be in Verse. We are to remember that the Psalms are Forms of our Addresses of Praise and Prayer to God : of whom and to whom nothing ought to be spoken, but with the highest veneration.

" The liberty of Connexion in this work is no more than what is usually taken in the litteral Prose-version of the Psalms. The same care has been taken to keep close to the Text, that its own proper vigour be not lost in too wide a Paraphrase. Doubtless it is not lawful for any one, to take, leave out, or add what they please; but adhering firmly to the Original, to transcribe the whole Truth; to raze out nothing but the Veil, which (as to us) was drawn before it. I have rejected the Verse of seven feet, as being worn out of use. I have made choice of the Verse of four or of five feet (one Psalm excepted), each following Verse giving the Rhime to the preceding; as seeming to me, more indifferent to be either Read or Sung than those of shorter and unequal lengths; or where the Rhime is alternate or of greater distance and they are more proper to be set for Church-Musick. The Verse composed of three feet will be too moving, and the Air set to it will be too light, for any subject which is in Dignity. So ought we to sever those Airs, which tend to Gayety and to Rapture. It were utterly needless to shew, how the Psalms, throughout all the Ages of Christianity, have been an express part of the Forms of Devotion. The Disciples oft sung them, and the Apostles after, and the same has been the undoubted Practice of the Christians throughout all Ages."

SIMON FORD, D.D.

1688.—A New Version of the Psalms of David in Metre, Smooth, plain and easie to the most ordinary capacities: by Simon Ford, D.D., Rector of Old Swinford, in Worcestershire. London, printed for Brabazon Aylmer, at the Three Pigeons over against the Royal Exchange.—*Brit. Mus. Lib.*

I.

"That man's an happy man indeed,
Whom ill advice doth not mislead :
    Nor doth he in that way remain,
Which men to sin accustom'd beat :
Nor sit, where haughty scorners treat
    Both God, and goodness, with disdain."

XXIII.

"The Lord my faithfull Shepherd is ;
Of nothing therefore can I miss,
    Which, to promote my good, I need :
In pastures fair He doth me place,
All overspred with tender grass,
    Where to the full He doth me feed."

Dr. Ford was born in Devonshire, 1619, and died in 1699. He explains his design : "I endeavoured to keep as near to the New Translation of the Psalmes, made in the Time, and by the command, of King James I."

JOHN PATRICK, D.D.

1691.—The Psalms of David in Meter. Fitted to the Tunes used in Parish Churches. By John Patrick, D.D., Preacher to the Charterhouse, London. Printed for John Churchill, at the Black Swan in Paternoster Row, and L. Meredith at the Star in St. Paul's Church Yard. (1694 edit.)—*Brit. Mus. Lib.*

I.

"Blest is the Man whose vertuous steps
    No wicked Counsels lead aside ;
Nor stands in Sinners ways ; nor sits
    Where God and Goodness men deride."

XXIII.

" God is my Shepherd, who will see
    That all my wants be still supply'd ;
I shall not be exposed to wrong,
    Nor left to stray without a Guide."

Dr. Patrick first published, in 1679, a "Century of
Select Psalms for the use of the Charter House." It
was republished in Hamburgh by T. Wierlag, in 1692 ;
and in 1694 an edition of the Psalms with about
twenty tunes was published. The latter has been
frequently reprinted.*

RICHARD BAXTER.

1692.—Mr. Richard Baxter's Paraphrase on the Psalms of David in
    Metre, with other Hymns, Left fitted for the Press under his
    own hand. Licensed June 2nd, 1692. London, printed for
    Thomas Parkhurst, at the Bible and Three Crowns in Cheap-
    side, near Mercer's Chapel.—*Brit. Mus. Lib.*

I.

" Blest is the man who doth avoid
    The counsel of ungodly mates ;
Who stands not in the sinners way,
    Nor sitteth in the scorners seats."

XXIII.

" The Lord Himself my Shepherd is,
    Who doth me feed and [safely] keep ;
What can I want that's truly good,
    While I am [one of] His own sheep ? "

* Mr. W. L. Taylor.

Baxter is well known as the author of "The Saint's Everlasting Rest," and other works. He was parish minister of Kidderminster, Chaplain to one of Cromwell's regiments, and subsequently one of the Court Chaplains to Charles II. That monarch offered to him the see of Hereford. After the passing of the Act of Uniformity he was a much-persecuted and imprisoned Nonconformist minister. His views have been called "Baxterian," a mild form of Calvinism. He drew up a reformed Liturgy when he was a member of the Savoy Conference for the revision of the Prayer-book. He was born in 1615, died in 1691.

Certain words in his lines are bracketed as capable of being omitted or retained, that his Psalms might be sung either in common or long measures. He claimed to be the inventor of the plan. "His poetic compositions sometimes lack finish, as he begrudged them the time necessary for their perfection, but they contain some fine passages." *

"I have in the end showed why I have done that which no man ever did before me, to fit the same Psalms to various Tunes and Measures, longer and shorter, specially to gratifie them by variety that are used to be dull'd with customariness in the same, and to give them expository notes who use but obscure abbreviation and conciseness in words, and I hope the Printer will make so visible a difference in the characters that the additional words shall stumble none" (Preface).

* "Our Hymns," by Josiah Miller, M.A.

The *family copy* of the 1692 edition is now in the collection of Mr. W. L. Taylor, of Peterhead.

TATE AND BRADY.

1696.—A New Version of the Psalms of David, Fitted to the Tunes used in Churches. By N. Tate and N. Brady. London, printed for the Company of Stationers. "To His Most Excellent Majesty William III. of Great Britain, France, and Ireland, King, Defender of the Faith, etc., this New Version of the Psalms of David is most Humbly dedicated by His Majesty's Most obedient subjects and servants."

Attached to this and the following editions was a copy of the Order in Council :—

"At the Court of Kensington, Dec. 3rd, 1696. Present, the King's Most Excellent Majesty in Council : Upon the humble Petitions of N. Brady and N. Tate this day read at the Board, setting forth that the Petitioners have, with their utmost care and industry, completed a New Version of the Psalms of David, in English Metre, fitted for public use ; and humbly praying his Majesty's Royal Allowance that the Version may be used in such congregations as may think fit to receive it : His Majesty, taking the same into his royal consideration, is pleased to order in Council, That the said New Version of the Psalms in English Metre, be, and the same is hereby Allowed and Permitted to be used in all Churches, Chapels, and Congregations, as shall think fit to receive the same. W. Bridgman." *

I.

"Happy the man whom ill advice
From virtue ne'er withdrew :
Who ne'er with sinners stood, nor sat
Amongst the scoffing crew."

* This first edition was recalled and destroyed on account of some objectionable passages.

XXIII.

"Since God does me, His worthless charge,
    Protect with tender care,
As watchful Shepherds guard their Flocks,
    What can I want or fear?"

Dr. Nahum Tate is described by Jacob as "a man of learning, candour, and courteous to all. He had a good share of wit, and a great deal of modesty, which prevented his making his fortune." He succeeded Shadwell as poet-laureate, was the author of several plays which were frequently acted in the last two decades of the seventeenth century, and died in poverty in the Mint in 1716.

Dr. Nicholas Brady, a zealous promoter of the Revolution of 1688, was Vicar of Richmond, Surrey, and held other benefices. His Psalms were translated at the Richmond Vicarage. Born 1659, died in 1726.

By a very long deed, dated December 3, 1696, Tate and Brady entered into partnership with the Stationers' Company for printing the new version of the Psalms, the copyright being divided into three great allotments of eighty shares each; with option of purchase by any one or more of the shareholders. The property, however, very soon after vested in the Stationers' Company.

In 1703 the Council at Hampton Court allowed and permitted a supplement to Tate and Brady, containing "the Psalms in Particular Measures, Hymns, Gloria Patria, etc.;" with appropriate tunes attached.

Montgomery thought the new version was nearly as inanimate as the Sternhold Psalter, though a little more refined.

LUKE MILBOURNE.

1698.—The Psalms of David in English Metre. Translated from the Original, and suited to all the Tunes now sung in Churches. By Luke Milbourne, a Presbyter of the Church of England. Dedicated to His Highness the Duke of Gloucester. London, printed for W. Rogers at the Sun, R. Clavell at the Peacock, and B. Tooke at the Middle Temple Gate, Fleet Street.— *Brit. Mus. Lib.*

I.

" A Thousand Blessings crown his Head,
Whose Heart all impious Counsel flies ;
And hates those paths where Sinners tread,
Who God, and all that's good, despise."

XXIII.

" He like a Shepheard, gently leads
My soul thro' Truth's delightful Ways ;
My foot sure by His Conduct treads,
And ne'er from Paths of Wisdom strays."

Milbourne calls himself an "ancient Presbyter of the Church of England." He was one of the authors satirized in Pope's "Dunciad." He was Rector of St. Ethelburga's, Bishopsgate, and Lecturer of St. Leonard's, Shoreditch. Died in 1720.

Pope said of his verses, "Dulness is sacred in a sound divine ;" and adds that "when Milbourne wrote against Mr. Dryden's 'Virgil,' he did him justice in printing at the same time his own intolerable translations."

Milbourne's preface is of historical value from the references to other versions. Mr. W. L. Taylor, who has in his possession a copy formerly in the collection of the late Dr. Bliss, says that it contains a manuscript note: "In Milbourne's Preface he mentions Burnaby and May's version—the first is published." May's version must have been seen by Milbourne in manuscript only.

CHARLES DARBY.

1704.—The Book of Psalms in English Metre. The Newest Version Fitted to the Common Tunes. By Charles Darby, Rector of Kedington, in Suffolk. London, printed for Thomas Parkhurst, at the Bible and Three Crowns in Cheapside.— *Brit. Mus. Lib.*

I.

"The man is blest, that walketh not
  With those that wicked are;
Nor in the way of Sinners stands,
  Nor sits in Scorners chair."

XXIII.

"The Lord Himself my Shepherd is,
  No want I need to fear:
In pastures green He makes me rest,
  Where pleasant waters are."

"I have aimed to keep as near as possible to the Words of the Text, without marring the Poetry; and when forced to depart from it, to keep as close as I could to the Sense, by expressing it in Words or Phrases equivalent. And so I leave it to the Censures of the Judicious"! (Preface).

DANIEL BURGESS.

1714.—Psalms, Hymns, and Spiritual Songs. By the late Rev. Mr. Daniel Burgess, Minister of the Gospel. London, printed for John Clark, at the Bible and Crown in the Old Change, near St. Paul's.—*Mr. W. L. Taylor's Collection.*

I.

" Blest is the Man, whom from God's Walk
  No ill Men lead aside ;
Who stands in no bad Way, nor sits
  Where Men God's Way deride."

XXIII.

" The Father, Son, and Holy Ghost,
  My gracious Shepherd is :
My Wants will always be supplied
  By tender Care of His.
As Shepherds find their helpless Flocks
  Places for Food and Rest ;
My ever-blessed Shepherd finds
  And leads me to the best."

Burgess was a popular preacher and author, minister of the Church meeting at New Court, Lincoln's Inn Fields. The Sacheverell mob gutted the meeting-house in 1710, and made a bonfire of its pulpit and other fittings. Swift ridiculed his oratory as " mixing unction with incoherence and ribaldry." A fairer estimate of his sermons was that they were "full of epigram, terse, quaint, clear, and never meaningless or dull."

"A truly spiritual Taste will keep well-disposed minds so intent to the Weight and Seriousness of the Matter, as not to leave them at leisure for little impertinent Criticisms upon the Phrase and Dress ; or the Exactness of Measure and Rhyme in these sacred Composures " (Preface by John Billingsley).

COTTON MATHER.

1718.—Psalterium Americanum. The Book of Psalms in a Translation Exactly conformed unto the Original ; but all in Blank Verse. Fitted unto the Tunes commonly used in our Churches, which pure offering is accompanied with Illustrations, digging for Hidden Treasures in it. Whereto are added some other portions of the said Scriptures, to enrich the cantonial. Boston, in N.E.—*Brit. Mus. Lib.*

I.

" What the blessings of the man
Who is not walking in
The counsel of the men that are
Set for impiety ? "

XXIII.

" My shepherd's the Eternal God ;
I shall not be in want ;
In pastures of a tender grass
He makes me to lie down."

" Our poetry," writes Mather, " has attempted many

versions of the Psalms, but they leave out a vast heap of those rich things which the Holy Spirit of God speaks in the original Hebrew ; and that they put in as large an heap of poor things, which are entirely their own. All this merely for preserving the Chink of the Rhyme. Some refining pieces of poetry, which this refining age has been treated withal, have been offered us in Blank Verse. And in Blank Verse we now have the Glorious Book of Psalms presented to us." This is one of the " rich things "—

> " As the Hart makes a panting cry
>   For cooling streams of waters ;
> So my soul makes a panting cry
>   To Thee, O mighty God ! "

Cotton Mather was born in 1663, died in 1728.

ISAAC WATTS, D.D.

1719.—* The Psalms of David imitated in the Language of the New Testament, and apply'd to the Christian State and Worship. By Dr. I. Watts. London.—*Brit. Mus. Lib.*

I.

> " Blest is the man who shuns the place
>   Where sinners love to meet ;
> Who fears to tread their wicked ways,
>   And hates the scoffers' seat."

* Dr. Watts's version was incomplete, lacking twenty of the Psalms. It was not until 1800 that Dr Timothy Dwight, President of Yale College, added the omitted Psalms to an edition published at the request of the General Association of Connecticut.

I

XXIII.

" My shepherd will supply my need,
    Jehovah is His Name ;
In pastures fresh He makes me feed,
    Beside the living stream."

Isaac Watts, D.D., Edinburgh and Aberdeen, 1728,
was the Independent minister of Berry Street Church,
London.   He was born in 1674, and died in 1748.
Several editions of Watts's Psalms were approved by
the Presbyterians in America, and were published in
Philadelphia, Charleston, Troy, and elsewhere.

" It is true that David has left us a richer variety
of Holy Songs than all that went before him," says
Dr. Watts ; "but rich as it is, 'tis still far short of the
glorious things that we Christians have to sing before
the Lord.   I could never persuade myself that the
best way to raise a devout frame in plain Christians
was to bring a King or a Captain into the Churches,
and let him lead and dictate the worship in his own
style of royalty or in the language of a field of battle.
Would I encourage a parish clerk to stand up in the
midst of a country church, and bid all the people
join with his words and say, ' I will praise Thee upon
a psaltery ;' or, ' I will open my dark sayings upon
the harp ' ?   I have chosen rather to imitate than to
translate, and thus to compose a Psalm-Book for
Christians after the manner of the Jewish Psalter."

" His ear was well tuned, and his diction was elegant and copious, but his devotional poetry is, like
that of others, unsatisfactory.   The paucity of its

topics enforces perpetual repetition, and the sanctity of the matter rejects the ornaments of figurative diction. It is sufficient for Watts to have done better than others what no man has done well " (Dr. Johnson).

SIR RICHARD BLACKMORE.

1721.—A New Version of the Psalms of David. Fitted to the Tunes used in Churches. By Sir Richard Blackmore, Kt., M.D. London, printed for the Company of Stationers. Certificated by the Archbishops of Canterbury and York, and seventeen Bishops, who recommended the King to give his Royal Allowance that the same be permitted to be used in all Churches, Chapels, and Congregations as shall think fit to receive the same. Agreed to by Order of Couneil, 27th October, 1720. —*Brit. Mus. Lib.*

I.

" O happy Man, who shuns all Day
 Th' Ungodly's Walks with Care ;
Who stands not in the Sinners' Way,
 Nor takes the Scorner's chair."

XXIII.

" God is my Shepherd, can I want ?
 He feeds me in the Meads ;
Do's for my rest green Pastures grant,
 And to still Waters leads."

Blackmore was physician to William III., born 1650, died 1729, author of several poems satirized by contemporary wits, who excelled in the habit.

" The lovers of musical devotion have always wished for a more happy metrical version than they have yet obtained of the Book of Psalms. This wish the piety of Blackmore led him to gratify; and he produced a new version of the Psalms of David, fitted for the tunes used in churches; which, being recommended by the archbishops and many bishops, obtained a licence for its admission into public worship; but no admission has yet been obtained, nor has it any right to come where Tate and Brady have got possession. Blackmore's name must be added to those of many others who, by the same attempt, have obtained only the praise of meaning well" (Dr. Johnson).

"The two classical poems of Blackmore and Milton ('Creation' and 'Paradise Lost') are more to be valued than all the poets, both of the Romans and the Greeks put together" (Hon. E. Howard : 1695).

Dennis, the poet, speaking of "Creation," said that it "equalled that of Lucretius in the beauty of its versification, and infinitely surpassed it in the solidity and strength of its reasoning."

CHARLES WESLEY.

1740.—A Poetical Version of nearly the whole of the Psalms of David. By the Rev. Charles Wesley, M.A. Edited by Henry Fish, M.A. London, John Mason, 1854. [Only a part of the Psalms in the Wesley Psalm and Hymn Book, 1740, were by Charles Wesley.]—*Brit. Mus. Lib.*

I.

"Bless'd is the man, and none but he,
    Who walks not with ungodly men;

Nor stands their evil deeds to see,
  Nor sits the innocent to arraign ;
The persecutor's guilt to share,
Oppressive in the scorner's chair."

XXIII.

" Jesus the good Shepherd is ;
  Jesus died His sheep to save ;
He is mine, and I am His ;
  All I want in Him I have.

.   .   .   .   .

Bear me to the sacred scene,
The silent streams and pastures green !
  Where the crystal waters shine,
  Springing up with life divine."

The stanza of the first Psalm is taken from the hymn-book

1744.—A Collection of Psalms and Hymns published by John and
    Charles Wesley.   Sold at the Foundry, Upper Moorfields.

That of the twenty-third Psalm from Mr. Fish's edition.

Charles Wesley, the hymn-writer of the Methodists—born 1708, died 1792—published during his lifetime as many hymns as would make ten ordinary volumes.   They were mainly founded upon the Psalms, the four Gospels, and the Acts of the Apostles.

SAMUEL PIKE.

1751.—The Book of Psalms in Metre. Fitted to the Various Tunes in Common Use : wherein Closeness to the Text, and Smoothness of the Verse, are preferred to Rhyme. With a prefatory account of the present Attempt, and some Thoughts on Social Worship. London, printed by H. Kent, and sold by J. Oswald, at the Rose and Crown in the Poultry, etc.—*Brit. Mus. Lib.*

I.

" Blessed, O blessed is the man
     Who wicked counsel shuns,
Nor stands not in the sinners way,
     Nor takes the scorners seat."

XXIII.

" The Lord Himself my Shepherd is,
     And I shall nothing want,
In pastures of the tender grass
     He makes me to lie down." *

The copy of this version, published anonymously, in the Lambeth Library has the name " H. Pyke " written on the title-page. Holland names the author " H. Pike." There is another edition in the British Museum Library, printed for G. Leighton, Vineyard Gardens, Clerkenwell, 1819.

"This version," says Dr. Cotton, "is in lyric measure, without rhyme; 'closeness to the text, and smoothness of the verse, are preferred to Rhyme.' It was published by Mr. Samuel Pike, minister of

---

* One of four translations of Ps. xxiii. Mr. Pike, in many cases, gives two or three versions of the same Psalm.

an Independent congregation in London. Afterwards he joined the Sandemanians, and became an eminent preacher among them. The version is still used in the worship of that religious sect."

Mr. Pike remarks, in his preface, "Not a few have long wished for a Version of the Psalms, etc., as close as might be to the original, freed from the objections of roughness of the lines, obsolete words, etc. . . . Upon the whole, it is apprehended that the following version is as close to the Scotch, or New England, and much smoother than either of them."

JOHN BARNARD.

1752.—A New Version of the Psalms of David, with several Hymns out of the Old and New Testament. Fitted to the Tunes used in the Churches. By John Barnard, Pastor of a Church at Marblehead. Boston, N.E., printed by J. Draper, for T. Leverett, in Cornhill.—*Brit. Mus. Lib.*

I.

" Thrice blest the man, who ne'er thinks fit
    To walk as wicked men advise ;
  To stand in sinners way, nor sit
    With those who God and man despise."

XXIII.

" The gracious Lord is still to me
    A Shepherd kind and faithful Guide ;
  Whate'er my Wants demand shall be,
    By his indulgent Care, supply'd."

Mr. Barnard's purpose was to improve the New

England version. All that an American biographer has to say about him is to record his birth in 1681, his death in 1770, and his being "distinguished for his sagacity in temporal affairs."

THOMAS CRADOCK, D.D.

1754.—A Poetical Translation of the Psalms of David from Buchanan's Latin into English Prose. By the Rev. Thomas Cradock, Rector of St. Thomas's Parish, Baltimore, Maryland. By permission of the Stationers' Company. London, printed for Mrs. Ann Cradock, at Wells, in Somersetshire, and sold by R. Ware, on Ludgate Hill.—*Brit. Mus. Lib.*

I.

" Blest is the man, whose honest soul disdains
    To tread the paths, where impious counsel reigns ;
    That in the way of sinners hath not stood,
    Nor fill'd the chair of the imperious proud."

XXIII.

" The bounteous Lord my pastures shall prepare,
    My God shall feed me with a shepherd's care ;
    In a fair verdant plain, with flow'rs o'erspread,
    Where Nature furnishes a velvet bed."

Cradock, who was a native of Staffordshire, died in 1760.

WHEATLAND AND SILVESTER.

1754.—The Psalms of David translated into Heroic Verse, in as Liberal a Manner as Rhyme and Metre will allow. With Arguments to each Psalm, and Explanatory Notes. Dedicated to His Royal Highness, George, Prince of Wales, etc., by Stephen Wheatland and Tipping Silvester. London, printed for S. Birt in Ave Mary Lane, and J. Buckland in Paternoster Row.—*Brit. Mus. Lib.*

I.

" Blessings await that man, who never strays
  Thro' wicked counsel from religion's ways ;
  From sinners' paths who keeps his cautious feet,
  And sits not vaunting in the scorners' seat."

XXIII.

" Jehovah tends me with a Shepherd's care,
  What pressing wants, what evil, can I fear ?
  At rest He in the verdant pasture lays,
  Or guides me, where the quiet current strays."

The authors, in their preface, after noting that Sir John Denham had said that he could have succeeded better in heroic verse, express the opinion—it " may vindicate the Use of it in this work, that it is intended for the Pocket, or the Closet, and not to be set to Church Music, or for the Publick worship."

FRANCIS HARE, D.D.

1755.—A New English Translation of the Psalms from the Original Hebrew, reduced to Metre by the late Bishop Hare ; . . . and a Preliminary Dissertation in which the Truth and Certainty of that learned Prelate's happy discovery is stated and proved at large.   By Thomas Edward, A.M., Fellow of Clare College, Cambridge.   Cambridge printed by J. Bentham, Printer to the University, for B. Dod, in Ave-Mary-Lane, London.—*Brit. Mus. Lib.*

I.

" How happy is the man who followeth not the Council of
    the wicked,
  Nor persisteth in the Way of Sinners,
  Nor sitteth in the assembly of scoffers ! "

XXIII.

  " Jehovah is my Shepherd,
    Therefore I shall want nothing ;
    He makes me to lie down in green pastures ;
    He leads me to soft-flowing waters."

Bishop Hare was educated at Eton and King's College, Cambridge, obtained successively the Deaneries of Worcester and St. Paul's, which latter office he held with that of the Bishopric of Chichester until his death in 1740.   He published an edition of " Terence," with notes.

THOMAS PRINCE.

1758.—The Psalms, Hymns, and Spiritual Songs of the Old and New Testament, faithfully translated into English Metre. Being the New England Psalm-Book Revised and Improved, by an Endeavour after a yet nearer Approach to the Inspired Original, as well as to the Rules of Poetry. By T. Prince. Boston, N.E., printed by Thomas and John Fleet, at the Heart and Crown in Cornhill.—*Brit. Mus. Lib.*

I.

" O Blessed Man who walks not in
　　The counsel of ill men,
Nor stands within the sinners way,
　　Nor scoffers seat sits in."

XXIII.

" The Lord Himself my Shepherd is,
　　Want therefore shall not I ;
He in the folds of tender grass
　　Soft makes me down to lie."

Thomas Prince was born in New England, educated at Harvard University, and was Pastor of South Church, Boston. His version met with general acceptance, successive editions being published. The first edition of his new Psalm-book reached a sale of thirty thousand copies.

GEORGE FENWICK.

1759.—The Psalter in its Original Form, or the Book of Psalms reduced to Lines, in an Easy and Familiar Style, and a Kind
of Blank Verse in Unequal Measures : answering for the most
part to the Original Lines, as supposed to contain each a
sentence, or some Entire part of one. With arguments, etc.
London, printed for T. Longman, in Paternoster Row.—*Brit.
Mus. Lib.*

I.

"I sing the Blessings which await the Man
Who ne'er in Counsel with the Wicked walks ;
Who does not in the way of Sinners stand ;
Nor in the Company of Scorners sit."

XXIII.

"My Shepherd is the Lord :
I cannot, therefore, want.
In fruitful fields He'll make me rest :
And lead me to refreshing Streams."

George Fenwick, B.D., was Rector of Hallaton,
Leicester. He writes, in his preface, "As to the
Attempt to reduce the sacred Hymns to Lines, in a
Kind of Blank Verse, it is on all hands confessed, I
think, that they were originally wrote in some such
Way, as an Help to Memory."

JAMES MERRICK.

1765.—The Psalms Translated or Paraphrased in English Verse. By
James Merrick, M.A., late Fellow of Trinity College,
Oxford. Reading, printed by J. Carnan & Co.—*Brit.
Mus. Lib.*

I.

"O how blest the Man, whose ear
Impious counsel shuns to hear,
Who nor loves to tread the way
Where the sons of Folly stray!"

XXIII.

"Lo! my Shepherd's hand divine!
Want shall never more be mine,
In a pasture fair and large
He shall feed His happy Charge."

Merrick—born 1720, died 1769—was the author of "The Camelion," and "The Destruction of Troy," translated into English metre from the Greek of Tryphiodoros. During his lifetime he tried to obtain the royal sanction, and failed; but in 1797 his version was formed into stanzas by W. D. Tattersall, and introduced in 1804, under the sanction of the king, into the parish church of Weymouth. Many other Tattersall editions followed.

Bishop Lowth said that Merrick was one of the best of men and most eminent of scholars. He took orders; but his delicate health prevented him from undertaking parochial work.

CHRISTOPHER SMART.

1765.—A Translation of the Psalms of David, attempted in the Spirit of Christianity, and Adapted to the Divine Service. By Christopher Smart, A.M., sometime Fellow of Pembroke Hall, Cambridge, and Scholar of the University. London. Printed by Dryden Leach for the author.—*Brit. Mus. Lib.*

I.

"The man is blest of God thro' Christ
    Who is not by the world intic't
        Where broader ruin lies ;
    Nor has descended to a seat
    Where scoffers at the gospel meet,
        Their Saviour to despise."

XXIII.

"The Shepherd Christ from heav'n arriv'd
    My flesh and spirit feeds ;
I shall not therefore be depriv'd
    Of all my nature needs.
As slop'd against the glist'ning beam
    The velvet verdure swells,
He keeps, and leads me by the stream
    Where consolation dwells."

"Kit Smart," as the eccentric poet was familiarly called, when composing his religious poems frequently wrote them upon his knees. His ruling passion was to repeat them, even when suffering from his temporary attacks of insanity. He was born in 1722, and died in 1770.

"In this translation," he remarks, in introducing his work to the notice of the reader, "all expressions that seem contrary to Christ are omitted ; and Evangelical matter put in their room,—and, as it was written with an especial view to the Divine Service, the reader will find sundry allusions to the rites and ceremonies of the Church of England, which are intended to render the work in general more useful and acceptable to Congregations."

REFORMED PROTESTANT DUTCH CHURCH PSALTER.

1767.—The Psalms of David, with the Ten Commandments, Creed, Lord's Prayer, etc., in Metre.   For the use of the Reformed Protestant Dutch Church of the City of New York.   New York, printed by James Parker, at the New Printing Office, in Beaver Street.—*Brit. Mus. Lib.*

I.

" How blest is he, who ne'er consents to walk
　By ill advice, nor dares to stand and talk
　In sinners' way, their Vice and Cause maintaining ;
Nor sits with Scorners, Things divine profaning ! "

XXIII.

" The Lord Himself doth condescend
　To be my Shepherd and my Friend :
　I on His faithfulness rely ;
His care shall all my want supply,
In pastures green He doth me lead,
And there in safety makes me feed,
　Refreshing streams are ever nigh,
　My thirsty soul to satisfy."

" The Consistory of the Reformed Protestant Dutch Church of New York, having, by Reason of the Declension of the Dutch Language, found it necessary to have Divine Service performed in their Church in English, Have adopted the following Version of the Psalms of David, which is greatly indebted to that of Dr. Brady and Mr. Tate ; some of the Psalms being transcribed verbatim from their version, and others altered, so as to fit them to the Music in the Dutch Churches." In this Psalter the musical score follows each line.

A version of the former Psalm-book, with a collection of hymns added, prepared, at the request of the Reverend Synod of the Reformed Dutch Church in North America, by Dr. John H. Livingston, Professor of Theology and Præces of the Synod, appeared in 1789: "The Psalms of David, with Hymns and Spiritual Songs. For the use of the Reformed Dutch Church in North America. New York, printed by Hodge, Allen, and Campbell, and sold at their respective Book Stores."

JAMES MAXWELL.

1773.—A New Version of the Whole Book of Psalms in Metre ; to which is added a Supplement of Divine Hymns and Scripture Songs. By James Maxwell, ·S. D. P. Glasgow. Printed by Wm. Smith for the Author.—*Brit. Mus. Lib.*

I.

"Bless'd is the man who keeps his feet
　　With care from sinners ways :
Who with the ungodly shuns to meet,
　　Nor with the scorner stays."

XXIII.

"The Lord's my Shepherd, by whose aid
　　My wants are all supply'd ;
Of what should I be then afraid
　　Since He's my constant guide ? "

The author says, addressing the ministers of the Church of Scotland, "Though I am satisfied this is the purest National Church at this day in the world ; yet I think there is still one thing still wants admendment amongst us ; namely, our Psalmody." He makes the "admendment" by substituting, for all allusions to "brutal sacrifices," the sacrifice of Christ, for references to "instrumental music," singing of grace with the heart, and he softens the imprecatory phrases. Maxwell was born in 1720, and died in 1800.

JOHN BARCLAY.

1776.—The Psalms Paraphrased according to the New Testament Interpretation, and adapted to the common Church Tunes. By John Barclay, A.M., Minister of the Berean Assembly, in Edinburgh. Sold by A. Donaldson, at his shop in St. Paul's Church Yard, and at Edinburgh by the Author.—*Brit. Mus. Lib.*

I.

" That man ! how great's his blessedness !
   And Jesus is the Man,
Who comes with perfect righteousness,
   The Holy peerless One ! "

XXIII.

" My God's my Shepherd, I'll not care
   For any breath of moved air ;
   The winds may blow, the storm may roar,
Jehovah will preserve his store."

Barclay—born 1734, died 1798—left the Church of Scotland, and became pastor of an independent congregation called " Bereans." His theological works were published in three volumes.

ROBERT BOSWELL.

1786.—The British Psalter. The Book of Psalms in Metre ; from the Original, compared with many Versions in different Languages. 2nd Edit. Printed for the Editor, and sold by J. Matthews, No. 18, Strand ; and C. Elliot, Edinburgh.— *Brit. Mus. Lib.*

I.

" O Greatly Blessed is the Man
Who walketh not astray
In counsel of ungodly men,
Nor stands in sinners way."

XXIII.

" The Lord's my Shepherd, I'll not want ;
He makes me down to lie
In pastures green,—He leadeth me
The quiet waters by."

The " British Psalter " first published in 1784, was used by the " Glassites," * of which denomination Boswell, a Writer to the Signet, was one of the teaching elders. He was an excellent Hebrew scholar. He was born in 1746, died in 1804.

The preface states that the version chiefly adhered to, as much the most literal, was the one then used by the Established Church of Scotland. The author endeavoured to improve the metre while retaining the literalness.

* Sandemanians in England, who sang out of Pike's version.

THE TINGSTADIUS VERSION.

1794.—The Psalms of David. A New and Improved Version. London, printed for M. Priestley (late Trapp), Paternoster Row, and J. Matthews, in the Strand, near Charing Cross.—*Brit. Mus. Lib.*

I.

" Happy is he !
That doth not follow the counsel of the unrighteous ;
Nor tread in the path of sinners ;
Nor sit in the assembly of the ungodly."

XXIII.

" The Lord is my Shepherd
I can want for nothing.
In meadows abounding in grass He leadeth me to pasture.
Near cooling places of repose to water."

This version was made from a translation of the Psalms by John Adam Tingstadius, D.D., Professor of Oriental Languages at the University of Upsal, by command of Gustavus III. of Sweden.

" If, as in many instances no doubt they will, the Psalms of David in their present garb appear to differ essentially from what we have hitherto been taught to consider as the real sentiments of the royal Psalmist, it is assumed that the alleged difference will not only have the advantage of sense and sound reason on its side, but be likewise found to correspond more faithfully with the original text " (Preface).

ELHANAN WINCHESTER.

1797.—The Psalms of David versified from a New Translation, and
adapted to Christian Worship.   Particularly intended for the
use of such Christians as believe in the universal and un-
bounded Love of God, manifested unto all His fallen creatures
by Christ Jesus.   London, printed for the Author, and sold
by Teulon, No. 100, Houndsditch ; Mr. Thrussel, Battle,
Sussex ; and at the Restoration Chapel, Parliament Court,
Artillery Lane, Bishopsgate Without.—*Brit. Mus. Lib.*

I.

" Prosperity attends my Lord,
   In ev'ry work, in ev'ry word,
      For He was in all good compleat ;
   He never unjust counsel took,
   And His great Father's love forsook,
      Or sat in the despiser's seat."

XXIII.

" Jesus my Lord and Shepherd is,
   Therefore I have no real want,
   But am in growing pastures fed ;
   By faith I taste the flowing blood,
   And drink of life's unceasing streams,
   From my Redeemer's wounded side."

The author was a celebrated universalist preacher,
previously minister of a chapel in Petticoat Lane,
1778–9. He translated the Psalms for "the more
especial use of such Christians whose eyes are by the
Divine Spirit enlightened to see the superabounding
love of the Father manifested by the gift of His Son,
for the redemption, salvation, and final glorification

of the whole of those unhappy beings whose sin has, or may yet draw from the allegiance, duty, and obedience due to their Creator."

JOSEPH COTTLE.

1801.—A New Version of the Psalms of David. By Joseph Cottle. London.—*Brit. Mus. Lib.*

I.

" How bless'd the men who walk with Thee,
 O Lord ! and prize what Thou hast said ;
Who both from sin and sinners flee,
 And shun the paths th' ungodly tread ! "

XXIII.

" Thou wilt, O God ! for me provide ;
 Thou art my shepherd and my guide ;
 Through pastures fair I take my way,
 And by the peaceful waters stray."

Cottle was for many years a bookseller in Bristol, and died at an advanced age in 1853. He is known as the author of " Recollections of S. T. Coleridge."

" I do not profess to have given a literal version of the Psalms. It was my object to catch the spirit rather than adhere to the letter. The abrupt pause, and sudden transition from one subject to another, are undoubted excellences in the writings of David, but which I thought could not be retained with advantage in a metrical version. I have therefore endeavoured to preserve a connected train of ideas, and have given, as much as possible, to each Psalm, the character of a whole."

THOMAS DENNIS.

1808.—A New Version of the Psalms in Blank Verse; with a Latin Version of the Eighth Psalm in Alcaic Verse. By the Rev. Thomas Dennis, Curate of Haslemere, Surrey. London, printed for J. White, Horace's Head, Fleet Street.—*Brit. Mus. Lib.*

I.

" Blest is the man who in the scorner's chair
 Hath never sat, nor with th'ungodly walk'd :
But his delight is in the law of God :
 That law his constant study."

XXIII.

" God is my Shepherd ; near refreshing streams,
 In pastures verdant with eternal spring,
He feeds me, and in safety makes me dwell."

" The version of the Psalms here offered to the public in Blank Verse, however defective and short of correctness and elegance it may be in that kind of composition, yet, perhaps, may not be unacceptable to many readers. A different dress and variety of diction may be pleasing to some persons, and be the means of supplying them with new sentiments of religious devotion " (Preface).

JOHN STOW.

1809.—A Version of the Psalms of David attempted to be closely accommodated to the Text of Scripture ; and adapted, by variety of measure, to all the Music used in the Versions of Sternhold and Hopkins and of Brady and Tate. By a Lay Member of the Church of England. London.—*Brit. Mus. Lib.*

I.

" Blest is the Man that walketh not
Where impious councel guides ;
Nor in the way of sinners stands,
Nor sits where Scorn presides."

XXIII.

" The Lord of heav'n my Shepherd is,
I therefore shall not want ;
And of salvation He the hope
Doth in my breast implant."

A third edition appeared in 1844, from which is copied the following unique dedication—probably, as Lowndes remarks, the only book ever dedicated to Jehovah * :—

* Mr. W. L. Taylor has a copy of the Scottish Psalms, with critical and explanatory notes, by Neil Douglas, Glasgow, 1815, dedicated to the Messiah. "To IMMANUEL, King of Kings, and Lord of Lords, his unworthy, but much obliged servant in the Gospel, Humbly presents, as in duty and gratitude bound, this work, undertaken with a single eye to his Glory, and for the defence and illustration of his truth, now finished, through the kindness of his providence, in believing hope of his Acceptance, divine patronage and blessing." Douglas describes himself as a " Preacher of Restoration."

TO THEE,

O! JEHOVAH!

THE ETERNAL

GODHEAD!

FATHER, SON AND HOLY GHOST!

THE INDIVISIBLE

TRINITY IN UNITY!

CREATOR, REDEEMER, SANCTIFIER

OF MANKIND!

WITH A LOWLY HEART AND WITH A TREMBLING HAND

THIS WORK

IS OFFERED:

IN THE HUMBLE HOPE

THAT, THROUGH THE INTERCESSORY OFFICES OF

THE EVER BLESSED JESUS,

AND THE SANCTIFYING OPERATIONS OF

THE HOLY SPIRIT,

(WHICH PROMPTED WHAT, IF ANY THING,

OF EXCELLENCE IT POSSESSES,)

IT MAY BECOME ACCEPTABLE BEFORE

THEE,

AND BE PERMITTED TO CONDUCE TO THE FURTHERANCE OF

THY GLORY

UPON EARTH,

AND THE ADVANCEMENT OF

THY KINGDOM

IN THE HEARTS OF

THY PEOPLE!

This dedication is not lost sight of in the new
arrangement of the Psalms, in which the verses are
designated as sung by the Psalmist to the congregation, by the congregation to each other, and by
each and all to Jehovah. This is Ps. xxiii. as arranged in the third edition :—

The Psalmist to the Congregation.

" 1. THE LORD of Heav'n my SHEPHERD is,
     I therefore shall not want;
For of His Care He doth the hope
     Within my breast Implant.

" 2. In pastures green He maketh me
     Lie down and calmly feed:
Beside the waters still and cool
     Me He doth also Lead.

" 3. He doth my Soul Restore, and will
     A Convert of it Make:
Me in the Paths of Righteousness
     HE Leads for His Name's sake.

To JEHOVAH.

" 4. Yea, tho' I walk thro' Death's dark vale
     I will no evil fear;
THY Rod and Staff, LORD, Aiding me,
     Do Comfort to me Bear.

" 5. For me a Table Thou Prepar'st
     Mine Enemies before;
With Oil my head Thou dost Anoint,
     The Cup too runneth o'er.

To the Congregation.

" 6. Goodness and Mercy surely shall
     Thro' life Attend me still:
And in the House of GOD the LORD,
     I will for ever dwell."

The British Museum copy is the one sent by the author to the Earl of Morton, January 10, 1810, with the request that he would, in his capacity of Lord Chamberlain, submit it to the Queen. Mr. W. L. Taylor has the copy sent by Stow to the Archbishop of Canterbury, who promised to send it or another to the Lambeth Library.

John Stow, of the Old South Sea House, and Croom's Hill, Greenwich, was the author of another curious work, "A Hermit's Narrative of Opinions, Many and Mighty, at Home and Abroad, and of his Solitary Meditations (spread over more than half a century of a life now entered upon the eighty-fifth year) on Divine Revelation and Christianity."

WILLIAM SAMUEL TOWERS.

1811.—A Version of the Psalms. By the late William Samuel Towers, Esq. Printed at the very particular request of several of the Author's friends. London.—*Brit. Mus. Lib.*

I.

"How blest the man, who all his days
    With caution shuns ungodly ways !
    Who ne'er with sinners will remain,
    Or scorners, who their Lord profane."

XXIII.

"Me, shall the Lord my Shepherd feed,
    Then nothing can I lack or need ;
    To pastures green He leads the way,
    Where constant streams of comfort stray."

WILLIAM GOODE.

1811.—An Entire New Version of the Book of Psalms; in which an attempt is made to accommodate them to the Worship of the Christian Church; with Original Prefaces and Notes. By the Rev. William Goode, M.A., Rector of St. Andrew Wardrobe, and St. Ann, Blackfriars. 2 vols. London.—*Brit. Mus. Lib.*

I.

" Happy the man who fears to stray
    Where men *ungodly* meet ;
Nor stand where *sinners* crowd the way ;
    Nor fills the *scorner's* seat."

XXIII.

" I hear my *Shepherd's* Voice,
    And in His care confide :
In THEE, JEHOVAH, I rejoice,
    My *wants* are all supplied.
Where *living pastures* grow,
    He bids me sweetly rest ;
Where *gentle streams* of *mercy* flow,
    My weary soul's refresht." *

In 1795 Goode was appointed to the living of St. Ann's, Blackfriars, and he held lectureships in other parishes of the City of London. His works, in six volumes, were edited and published by his son in 1822. He was born in 1762, died in 1816.

He proposed to make a version simple enough for the people generally, and adapted to the Christian dispensation.

* Goode wrote four versions of Ps. xxiii.

ROBERT DONALD.

1815.—The Psalms of David on Christian Experience. By R. D., Woking, Surrey. Guildford Press.—*Brit. Mus. Lib.*

I.

" That happy man is truly blest
    With the unholy have no rest,
    Who hates the sinner's scoffing seat ;
    But with the godly longs to meet."

XXIII.

" The Shepherd chief of Israel is,
        Jesus my Lord and King ;
    For well He knows each sheep of His
        Them to the fold will bring.
    He leads them safe to pastures green,
        Beside the living brook :
    Clear as the crystal to be seen,
        Their names in his fair book."

" The following is a feeble attempt (of a weak instrument in the hand of the Lord) on the Psalms of David. I, the author, first felt the power of a call either in the *Evangelical* or the *Gospel Magazine*, I do not recollect which, about five or six years ago ; it was a request to have a new publication of the Psalms, on Christian Experience (if I mistake not) in imitation of Cowper or Newton, when these words came powerfully into my mind, ' Thou art the man ! ' " (Preface).

G. F. HOLFORD, M.P.

1820.—The Book of Psalms in Verse ; with a short Explanatory Preface
to each Psalm, taken from the Works of Different Writers on
the Psalms, but chiefly from Bishop Horne's Commentary.
London, sold by Rivingtons and Hatchards. Printed by the
Philanthropical Society, St. George's Fields. (2nd Edit.
1822.)—*Brit. Mus. Lib.*

I.

" Blest he of men, who ne'er hath turn'd aside
  To walk with sinners, and the truth deride ;
  But makes the law of God his chief delight,
  There reads by day, and meditates by night."

XXIII.

" The Lord, my Shepherd, doth each want supply.
  In pastures green He causeth me to lie ;
  My feet by cooling streams He deigns to guide,
  And leads me where the peaceful waters glide."

In the copy in the British Museum Library, the
name of the author is queried as " By G. F. Holford,
M.P. ? "

The author believes that the language in which he
has expressed the Psalms is such that the common
people may very well understand ; and that his version,
with its prefaces and notes, will prove very useful to
young people.

Mr. W. L. Taylor's copy has on its fly-leaf, " To
Louisa T. Clare, from R. S. Holford." It also contains
a manuscript note by a former owner, " This is
Holford's version."

WILLIAM COLDWELL.

1821.—The Book of Praises. The Psalms or Sacred Odes of the Royal Psalmist David, and others the Prophets of Jehovah, in Metre. By William Coldwell, London.—*Brit. Mus. Lib.*

I.

" Blessed, write that man, supremely, who amidst
The counsel walks not of the impious ones ;
Nor in the paths of sinners stands ; nor sits,
Delighted with the scornful."

XXIII.

" My Shepherd is JEHOVAH ! I shall know
No deficiency ; in pastures verdant
I couch, by Him led beside placid waters."

Coldwell paraphrased the whole of the Psalms in blank verse, but only published the first part. He resided at Sheffield, was a geological surveyor and architect, and a local preacher in the Methodist New Connexion. The preface to his version intimates that he had originally attempted a version in rhyme, but did not succeed in satisfying himself. Afterwards he tried blank verse. He also published several works on different subjects.

BASIL WOODD.

1821.—A New Metrical Version of the Psalms of David, with an Appendix of Select Psalms and Hymns. By the Rev. Basil Woodd, M.A., of Trinity College, Oxford. London.—*Brit. Mus. Lib.*

I.

" Blest is the man whose heav'n-taught mind
    Disdains the paths which scorners find,
    The law of GOD, his chief delight,
    He meditates by day and night."

XXIII.

" My Shepherd is the Lord,
    I never more shall want ;
All I require, my gracious GOD
    Will mercifully grant.
    In meadows fair and green,
    With purest pasture blest ;
Where the still waters gently flow,
    He leadeth me to rest."

Basil Woodd was an Evangelical clergyman, Rector of Drayton Beauchamp, in Buckinghamshire. Died in 1831, aged seventy-one. He says, in his introductory remarks, " It has been a principal object in the following attempt to preserve, where it was practicable, the expressions of the authorized translations, to accommodate the sentiments to the language of the Christian Dispensation, and to direct the mind, when the subject authorized, to the life, death, resurrection, and glory of the Lord Jesus Christ."

JAMES MONTGOMERY.

1822.—Songs of Zion ; being Imitations of the Psalms. By James Montgomery. London, Longmans, etc.—*Brit. Mus. Lib.*

I.

"Thrice happy he, who shuns the way
    That leads ungodly men astray ;
    Who fears to stand where sinners meet,
    Nor with the scorner takes his seat."

XXIII.

"The Lord is my Shepherd, no want shall I know ;
    I feed in green pastures, safe-folded I rest ;
    He leadeth my soul where the still waters flow,
    Restores me when wandering, redeems when opprest."

"The author pretends not to have succeeded better than any that have gone before him ; but, having followed in the track of none, he would venture to hope, that, by avoiding the rugged literality of some, and the diffusive paraphrases of others, he may, in a few instances, have approached nearer than either of them have generally done, to the ideal model of what devotional poems, in a modern tongue, grounded upon the subjects of ancient Psalms, yet suited for Christian edification, ought to be."

James Montgomery was born in 1771, died in 1854. Editor, printer, and author of "Greenland" and other poems. Up to middle age not a "stated" member of any religious community. In 1814, however, he rejoined the Moravians, among whom he had received his early education. The town of Sheffield gave the poet a public funeral.

JAMES USHER.

1823.—A New Version of the Psalms ; principally from the Text of Bishop Horne. By James Usher. Printed and Published by the Author, Buckley Street, Whitechapel. Dedicated to the Rev. Robert Hamilton, D.D., "the venerable preceptor under whom I received the most part of my very moderate education."—*Brit. Mus. Lib.*

I.

" Oh ! how he's blest who'll not consent
    In ways of guile to walk,
Nor will the seats of those frequent
    Who blasphemously talk."

XXIII.

" God is my Shepherd, lack I've none ;
He to green pastures leads me on ;
And will to streams of comfort guide,
Convert my soul, and grace provide."

" The public are here presented with the musings of a man of leisure, who has long made the Psalmes his daily study ; although the present must be acknowledged rather a hasty production, having been begun on the 18th August last, and finished on the 15th December " (Preface).

He claims to have restrained his fancy and kept near the text.

BAPTIST NOEL TURNER.

1824.—Songs of Solyma ; or a New Version of the Psalms of David,
the long ones being compressed in General into Two Parts,
or Portions of Psalmody; comprising their Prophetic Evi-
dences and Principal Beauties.   By Baptist Noel Turner,
M.A., Rector of Denton, in Lincolnshire, and Wing, in
Rutland.   London, Rivingtons.—*Brit. Mus. Lib.*

I.

"Blest is the man whose wary steps
    All sinful paths decline ;
Who most avoids those impious men
    That scoff at things divine."

XXIII.

"The Lord my pasture shall prepare,
    And feed me with a shepherd's care ;
His presence shall my wants supply,
    And guard me with a watchful eye." *

A memoir and portrait of Baptist Noel Turner—
born 1739, died 1826—is in Nicholl's "Illustrated
History."   In early life he was known to, and much
esteemed by, Dr. Johnson.

"The hope of adapting the Psalms to the purpose
of Congregational Singing, in a manner somewhat
preferable to that generally in use, may be regarded
as having given origin to the present little work."
The author also states in his preface that he "had
become an octogenarian before the commencement
of the present work."

* Addison's : one of the four in Turner's Psalter not original, but
stated to be "from Addison, slightly altered."

"These translations are highly respectable in point of literary merit, particularly when it is considered that they were the amusements of the evening of a literary life, the author having attained his eightieth year when he began the task" (*Gentleman's Magazine*).

RICHARD MANT, D.D.

1824.—The Book of Psalms, in an English Metrical Version, Founded on the basis of the Authorised Bible Translation, and compared with the Original Hebrew; with Notes Critical and Illustrative. By the Right Rev. Richard Mant, D.D., M.R.I.A., Lord Bishop of Down and Connor. Oxford, J. Parker. London, Rivingtons.—*Brit. Mus. Lib.*

I.

"How blest is he, who shuns the road,
　By impious men perversely trod;
Nor his to stand, where sinners meet;
　Nor his the graceless scorner's seat!"

XXIII.

"My shepherd is the Lord Most High;
　His care shall all my wants supply;
Lay me in pastures green to feed,
　And to the tranquil steamlet lead."

Dr. Mant was born in 1776, died in 1848; Rector of St. Botolph's, Bishopsgate, 1816; Rector of East Horsley, 1818; Bishop of Killaloe, 1820; Down and Connor, 1823; and Dromore, 1842. He was a voluminous author. He published his great work, "The History of the Church of Ireland," in 1840.

"I beg that I may be distinctly understood as not pretending to offer a Version of the Psalm *new* in any other signification than in that of the form wherein it is offered " (Preface).

"Bishop Mant's hymns are not free from the defects that usually mark works produced in haste, in a life crowded with conflicting duties, and erring in excess of literary production " (Miller).

The *Dublin University Magazine*, however, expresses the opinion that Mant's version is both the most instructive and the most poetical version of the Psalms published up to that time.

MATTHEW SANKEY.

1825.—A New Version of the Psalms of David, dedicated to the Archbishop of Cashel. By Matthew Sankey, Esq. Printed for C. and J. Rivington.—*Brit. Mus. Lib.*

I.

"O happy is the man, that ne'er
    In counsel with the ungodly walk'd ;
Nor stood with sinners, nor that e'er
    Hath sat where impious scorners talk'd."

XXIII.

"The Lord, my shepherd is indeed,
    That doth my wants supply ;
In pastures green He makes me feed,
    And by still waters lie."

"I have generally," says Mr. Sankey, "followed the metres of the New Version, having an eye to the beautiful Church music."

EDWARD ROWLAND.

1826.—The Psalms of David, attempted in Verse, regular, irregular, in the way of paraphrase, etc. By Senex, a Clergyman. Carlisle, printed by Charles Thurnham, Market Place.— *Brit. Mus. Lib.*

I.

" Blessed is he that hath not walk'd
As wicked men advise,
Nor wandered in the paths of vice,
Where pride and scorn arise."

XXIII.

" His tender flock the careful shepherd leads,
Unto cool waters and to verdant meads ;
So doth the mighty shepherd of the soul,
My wants supply, my wanderings controul."

Rowland was a retired timber-merchant, who is said to have taken holy orders after he left business. He died in 1824, aged eighty-one.

Most of his Psalms are in elegaic stanzas.

JOHN MAULE, M.D.

1827.—A New Version of the Psalms of David, by John Maule, M.D. Marlborough, published by W. W. Lucy.—*Mr. W. L. Taylor's Collection.*

I.

" Blest is the man who turns aside
From every evil path with care ;
Whom wicked councils ne'er seduce,
Who, watchful, shuns the scorner's chair."

XXIII.

" My shepherd is the living Lord,
    I nothing therefore need ;
  In pastures fair, near pleasant streams,
    He setteth me to feed."

The only note in this volume contains the following : " The author takes this opportunity of offering his best thanks to his subscribers, and trusts that the extra charge of one shilling per copy will not be thought unreasonable."

MARGARET PATULLO.

1828.—The Christian Psalter ; a New Version of the Psalms of David, calculated for all Denominations of Christians. By Margaret Patullo, Perth. Edinburgh, printed for the Author.—*Brit. Mus. Lib.*

I.

" Happy the man who loves the Lord
    With his whole heart and soul ;
  God numerous mercies will afford,
    For He does all control."

XXIII.

" O Lord of Glory, us preserve,
    And from all ill defend—
  Thou art the Saviour whom we serve,
    Who constant peace can send.
  Beside quiet waters Thou wilt guide
    Me, gently to repose,
  And lead me to the cool shade
    Where tender green grass grows."

The only complete metrical Psalter composed by a lady. Miss Patullo was a Scotchwoman of good family in Perthshire. She held that the name of our Lord and Saviour Jesus Christ ought not to be omitted in spiritual Psalms.

WILLIAM WRANGHAM.

1829.—A New Metrical Version of the Psalms; adapted to Devotional Purposes. By W. Wrangham. London, Simpkin, Marshall, and Co.—*Brit. Mus. Lib.*

I.

" Blest is the man, whose perfect heart
From virtue never strays;
Who from the scorner keeps apart,
And shuns the sinner's ways."

XXIII.

" My watchful Shepherd is the Lord,
On whom for shelter I rely;
His love shall constant aid afford,
His bounty all my wants supply;
He bids me feed in pastures green,
Where peaceful streams adorn the scene."

The object of the writer—a tradesman of Louth, in Lincolnshire, who died in 1832—was to produce a metrical version of the Psalms in such language and so arranged so as to render it suitable to general parochial psalmody. The measures were intended to be correspondent to those which are usually sung in churches.   The version was printed at Louth, in Lincolnshire.

WALTER JOHN TROWER, D.D.

1831.—A New Metrical Psalter, first published in 1831, now revised and republished by W. J. Trower, D.D., Bishop, Rector of Ashington, and Sub-dean of Exeter.   Oxford and London, James Parker and Co.   (Edit. 1875.)—*Brit. Mus. Lib.*

I.

"Bless'd who away from counsels good
    Hath never turn'd his feet;
Nor in the way of sinners stood,
    Nor shar'd the scorner's seat."

XXIII.

"My shepherd is the Lord,
    Therefore no want I know;
He in green pastures doth me feed,
And by the hand doth gently lead
    Where the still waters flow."

The author wished, not only to express faithfully the sense of the sacred writers of the Book of Psalms, but to express it as much as possible in the language we are so familiar with in the Bible and Common Prayer-book versions.   He occasionally allowed himself considerable harshness of metre rather than give up the words and the cadences to which long use had attached him.

Dr. Trower was Bishop of Glasgow and Galloway.

ALFRED BARTHOLOMEW.

1831.—Sacred Lyrics: being an Attempt to Render the Psalms of David more applicable to Parochial Psalmody. By Alfred Bartholomew, Architect. London, Rivingtons.—*Brit. Mus. Lib.*

I.

" That man is bless'd who dares despise
   What sinful mortals falsely prize ;
   Who can divest, by reason calm,
   Fair false advice of every charm ;
   Who though persuasion tempts him, shuns
   The pathway that to ruin runs."

XXIII.

" The Lord my Shepherd—favour'd care—
   Through every hour I kindness share.

.   .   .   .   .

   In pastures ever verdant fed,
   Beside the streams of comfort led,—
   God will at length my soul convert,
   And all my steps from sin divert."

EDWARD GARRARD MARSH.

1832.—The Book of Psalms translated into English Verse, and Illustrated with Practical and Explanatory Notes. By Edward Garrard Marsh, M.A. London, Seeleys.—*Brit. Mus. Lib.*

I.

" How blest the man, who shuns the tents
   Where impious councils meet,
Who ne'er the sinner's haunts frequents,
   Nor fills the scorner's seat."

XXIII.

" I will Jehovah for my Shepherd hail ;
    For, while He feeds me, I shall never fail.
    In verdant pastures He will lay me down,
    By springs of comfort lead me, as His own."

The annotations, or explanatory notes, fill more than two hundred pages of the book.

Mr. Marsh was a clergyman, Minister of Hampstead Chapel.

HENRY GAHAGAN.

1832.—A Rhyme Version of the "Liturgy" Psalms. By Henry Gahagan, Esq., M.A., Barrister-at-Law. London, Rivingtons.—*Brit. Mus. Lib.*

I.

" That man is blessed, who will never tread
    In paths by counsel of th' ungodly led ;
    Who in his way the sinner will not meet,
    Nor with the scornful deign to take his seat."

XXIII.

" The Lord's my Shepherd—I His sheep
    Can nothing lack, while in His keep ;
    In green pastures shall He feed me,
    To refreshing waters lead me."

" This work has no pretensions to be taken as a Metrical Translation of the Psalms, but is strictly, as I have entitled it, a Rhyme Version of our 'Liturgy' Psalms" (Preface).

JOSEPH P. BARTRUM.

1833.—The Psalms Newly Paraphrased for the Service of the Sanctuary. By Joseph P. Bartrum. Designed chiefly as a Supplement to Sacred Lyrics in use. Boston, Russell, Odiorne, and Co.—*Philadelphia Library.**

I.

"Where shall happiness be found?
   Heaven replies—O Welcome sound!—
Happy who from sin depart,
Turn from every treach'rous art!
Who, intent on truth divine,
Read by day the hallow'd line;
Ponder still the page by night;
Linger o'er it with delight."

XXIII.

"The Lord is my Shepherd benign!
   No want shall distress me, nor woe!
He leads me to pastures divine,
   By rivers that peacefully flow!
Ah! tempted too often to stray,
   He rescues from error and sin;
Restores me to virtue's bright way,
   A crown everlasting to win."

The author says, "Acquainted with no metrical version of the Psalms combining chasteness of interpretation with an application to existing manners, and sublimity of language with a fitness for devotional music, I venture to make an offering to the public, in the hope of supplying a deficiency."

* For these extracts, and those of G. Burgess, McClure, and D. C. McLaren, the author is indebted to Mr. B. Samuel, of the Ridgway Branch of the Library Company of Philadelphia.

GEORGE MUSGRAVE.

1833.—The Book of the Psalms of David, in English Blank Verse;
being a New Poetical Arrangement of the Sweet Songs of
Israel: adapted to the use of general Readers, with a view
to the more perfect understanding, and consequent relish and
appreciation, of the subject-matter of those Divine Compositions. By the Rev. George Musgrave, A.M., B.N.C., Oxon.
London, Rivingtons.—*Brit. Mus. Lib.*

I.

" Blessed is he whose mortal life's career
   Its onward course maintaineth unapproach'd
   Of sin's unhallow'd counsel, and whose feet
   Untrodden leave the devious paths of guilt."

XXIII.

" In God HIMSELF my Shepherd I behold—
   Henceforth to live unconscious of a want;
   For, by His heavenly guidance led, I rest
   In pastures verdant with the tend'rest grass."

The author, born in 1798, was formerly Curate of
Marylebone, and spent the latter part of his life in
literary and scientific pursuits.

" The version here given, though little more than a
synonymous and poetical repetition of the sense of
the text, may exhibit this single advantage at least—
that the portion of Scripture it involves, being rendered in different terms from those to which the ear
of the many has been accustomed, will, in a variety
of instances, appear in a new light, and sharpen a
blunted attention " (Preface).

P. J. DUCAREL.

1833.—A Paraphrase of the Psalms, executed in Blank Verse; with strict attention to the Notes and Commentaries of Bishops Horsley, Horne, etc. By P. J. Ducarel, Esq. London, Hamilton, Adams, and Co.—*Brit. Mus. Lib.*

I.

"Blessed is he, who from his steadfast course
  Ungodly counsels shall not lead astray;
  Who, with the sinners lingers in his path,
  Nor sits in mockery in the scorner's seat."

XXIII.

"God is my Shepherd, and beneath His care,
  I can lack nothing; His Almighty hand
  'Midst fairest meadows of luxuriant green,
  Shall pasture me, and shall conduct my steps
  Where the sweet springs of balmy comfort flow."

"The object of the following paraphrase is to give more connection and continuity of meaning to each composition, as presented in the language of our Bible and Prayer-book" (Preface).

H. A. S. ATWOOD.

1834.—A New Version of the Book of Psalms, adapted to the purpose of Congregational Psalmody. By the Rev. H. A. S. Atwood, M.A., Curate of Kenilworth. Coventry, printed for the Author.—*Brit. Mus. Lib.*

I.

" Blest is the man, who shuns the seat
 Of scorners, and from paths of vice
With pious care restrains his feet,
 Who from his God no snares entice."

XXIII.

" Where smile the pastures ever green,
 Where cooling waters flow,
Where plenty crowns the fruitful scene,
 My Shepherd bids me go."

" In preparing this Version," the author says, " a leading object has been to comprise as much as possible the spirit of the whole Psalm, within the compass of the few Verses usually devoted to Congregational singing, dividing the very long Psalms into two, or more parts."

HENRY FRANCIS LYTE.

1834.—The Spirit of the Psalms, or the Psalms of David adapted to Christian Worship. By the Rev. H. F. Lyte, A.M., Minister of Lower Brixham. London, William Marsh.— *Brit. Mus. Lib.*

I.

" How blest are they who fear to walk
 Where sinners tempt, and scorners talk,
 Who in the Word of God delight,
 And feed upon it day and night ! "

XXIII.

"The Lord of all my Shepherd is;
What can I want, while I am His?
In greenest fields my soul He feeds,
My steps by stillest waters leads."

Lyte was born in 1793; died, at Nice, 1847; Perpetual Curate of Brixham, 1823; author of the popular hymn "Abide with Me" and other religious poetry.

Lyte wrote that he had "endeavoured to give the spirit of each Psalm in such a compass as the public taste would tolerate, and to furnish, sometimes, when the length of the original would admit of it, an almost literal translation, sometimes a kind of spiritual paraphrase, at others even a brief commentary of the whole Psalm."

WILLIAM ALLEN, D.D.

1835.—Psalms and Hymns for Public Worship, containing all the Psalms and Hymns of Dr. Watts which are deemed valuable. Together with a New Version of all the Psalms and many Original Hymns, besides a large Collection from other Writers. By William Allen, D.D., President of Bowdoin College. Boston, W. Pierce.—*Mr. W. L. Taylor's Collection.*

I.

"Blest is the man, whose feet ne'er stray,
Misguided by Advice unmeet;
Who stands not in the sinner's way,
Nor sits in daring scoffer's seat."

XXIII.

"The Lord my Shepherd is, on high;
　To every want He brings supply,
　In pastures green He gives repose,
　And leads, where living water flows."

Dr. Allen "deems a new Psalm and Hymn Book necessary, in the present improved state of the public taste, for the purposes of Congregational worship. He has endeavoured to meet the claims of the public taste, and the wants of the Churches. In his version of Psalms he uniformly studied the Psalm, and endeavoured to catch its spirit, without any reference to other versions. Nor does he recollect that, except in one or two instances, he has borrowed a line from any author; though, doubtless, his memory may have unconsciously furnished him with a few lines borrowed from others. Never in a Psalm or Hymn has he been willing to sacrifice sense to sound; nor does he conceive that the necessity of rhyme has impaired the sentiment."

The following are additional versions :—

I.

"That man is blest alway,
　Who shuns advice unmeet,
Who stands not in the sinner's way,
　Nor sits in scorner's seat."

"Blest is he, whose prudent feet
　Sinners' bypaths ne'er have known,
Blest, who in the scorner's seat
　Ne'er with blasphemy sits down."

XXIII.

" My Shepherd is the Lord, my God,
    No want I e'er shall know ;
Guided by Him, my feet have trod
    Where greenest pastures grow."

"God's my Shepherd, and His eye,
    Sleepless, watches o'er my soul ;
While His rod and crook are nigh,
    I am safe, though wild beasts prowl."

"Christ, my Shepherd, is my guide,
    All my wants shall be supplied ;
He doth make me to repose
    Where the green, sweet pasture grows."

" My Shepherd ! my soul He will feed ;
    In folds of green grass I repose,
In pastures most sweet do I feed,
    I'm led by the stream that soft flows."

"The Lord is my Shepherd, I never shall need,
    In greenness of pasture He maketh me feed ;
He leadeth my soul by the still waters' side,
    Where streams of salvation most gently do glide."

E. FARR.

1836.—A New Version of the Psalms of David, in all the Various Metres suited to Psalmody, divided into Subjects, designated according to Bishop Horne, etc. By E. Farr. London, published by H. Fellowes, Ludgate Hill.—*Brit. Mus. Lib.*

I.

"How happy is the man whose feet
  Turn from the counsels of the base;
Who standeth not where sinners meet,
  Nor with the scorners takes his place!"

XXIII.

"The Lord is my Shepherd divine,
  No want shall I e'er undergo;
Thro' Him I in quiet recline,
  Where pastures abundantly grow."

"I have divided those Psalms which comprise more than one subject. . . . I have also endeavoured to make each portion perfect in itself, without transposing the sense of the original, adapting, to the best of my judgment, the metre to the subject, and using all the various metres" (Preface).

"A very successful recasting into metre of the substance of the Authorized Version," writes Mr. Holland, who somewhat depreciatingly calls the author "an individual of the name of Farr."

CATHERINE FOSTER AND ELIZABETH COLLING.

1838.—A New Metrical Version of the Psalms of David. By C. F. and E. C. London, Simpkin, Marshall, and Co.—*Brit. Mus. Lib.*

I.

"Blest is the man that hath not trod,
    The sinners' downward way;
Nor sought, forgetful of his God,
    Their friendship's fatal sway,
Who shuns the councils where they meet,
And sits not in the scorner's seat."

XXIII.

"The Lord my Shepherd still hath been,
    No want shall then be mine;
He bids me feed in pastures green,
    In the cool meads recline."

"A New Rhyme Version is still a desideratum in the language," wrote the authors. "Those who have adhered to the literal have allowed the poetical to escape, and those who have studied the poetical have wandered too far from the literal. An attempt has here been made to unite as much as it was possible the two. . . . Primarily intended for the Closet, but most of them will admit of being adapted to the Church."

JOHN KEBLE.

1839.—The Psalter, or Psalms of David, in English Verse. Adapted for the most part to Tunes in common use. By a Member of the University of Oxford. Oxford, John Henry Parker; London, Rivingtons.—*Brit. Mus. Lib.*

I.

" How blest the man who never trod
    Where sinners haunting wait,
Stood in the way with foes of God,
    In scorners' council sate ! "

XXIII.

" My Shepherd is the Lord ; I know
    No care or craving need ;
He lays me where the green herbs grow
    Along the quiet mead."

He was born in 1792, died in 1866 ; Fellow of Oriel
College, Oxford, and Vicar of Hursley, near Winchester. Keble was the author of " The Christian
Year," which attained so large a sale that the church
at Hursley was partly rebuilt out of the profit of it.

" It is not without very great misgiving and re-
luctance that this version of the Psalms is published ;
such misgiving as would yield to no sanction short of
what it has been honoured with. It was undertaken,
in the first instance, with a serious apprehension that
the thing attempted is, strictly speaking, *impossible*,
it being obvious, from the structure of the Hebrew
Psalms, that they were intended, not for singing, but
for chanting. . . . The object which has been chiefly
kept in view in preparing the present version has
been to express the effect of each Hebrew clause by
a single line instead of half a stanza, at the risk, too,
often, of a harshness and constraint, both in sound
and expression."

GEORGE BURGESS, D.D.

1840.—The Book of Psalms translated into English Verse. By *George Burgess, A.M.,* Rector of Christchurch, Hartford, Conn. New York, F. J. Huntington and Co.—*Philadelphia Library.*

I.

" How bless'd the man, who will not stray
　　Where godless counsels tempt his feet ;
　Who stands not in the sinner's way ;
　　Who sits not in the scorner's seat ! "

XXIII.

" The Lord is my Shepherd ; I ne'er shall have need :
　He gives me my couch in the green, quiet mead ;
　He leads me beside the still waters ; and brings
　His wand'rer to pathways where righteousness springs."

Dr. Burgess became Bishop of Maine, American Protestant Episcopal Church, in 1847. Born in 1809, he died at sea in 1866, when returning home from the West Indies.

In his preface he writes, " In the present version the author has endeavoured to follow the same principles which would govern him in the translation of any ancient poems into English verse ; to be so literal as to give the very sentiment, and, if possible, the spirit of the original, and yet so free as not to inflict pain on the reader of taste. If he has failed, he may say with Mr. Goode, ' it will be his solace that he has failed amongst names the most respectable in the annals of piety and literature.' He will but have made an unsuccessful attempt in a region where the very attempt was more delightful than success in other fields."

JOHN EDEN.

1841.—The Book of Psalms in Blank Verse, with Practical Reflections, by the *Rev. John Eden, B.D.*, late Vicar of St. Nicholas' and St. Leonard's, Bristol.   Hamilton Adams and Co.—*Sion College Library.*

I.

" Blest is the man whose feet have never walk'd
　 In the ungodly's counsel, never trod
　 In the transgressor's path ; who ne'er hath sat
　 Where sit the scornfull."

XXIII.

" God is my Shepherd ; therefore shall my soul
　 Lack nothing.   He shall give me to repose
　 In verdant pastures ; He shall lead me forth
　 Beside refreshing streams."

He was forty-one years Vicar of St. Nicholas'—from 1799 to his death in 1840—having previously been a Minor Canon of Bristol Cathedral.

The editor's preface states, "With respect to the performance itself, it is distinguished from nearly all the numerous versions which have preceded it, by the peculiarity of its execution in continuous heroic verse, without the division of stanzas or the accompaniment of rhyme."

FRANCIS SKURRAY.

1843.—A Metrical Version of the Book of Psalms, composed for Private Meditation or Public Worship. By Francis Skurray, B.D., Rector of Winterbourne, Steepleton, Dorset. London, William Pickering.—*Brit. Mus. Lib.*

I.

" Blest is the man, who all his days,
　　From evil paths hath kept his feet,
And never stood in sinners' ways,
　　Nor ever sat where scorners meet."

XXIII.

" The Shepherd shall my footsteps lead
　　From barren rock to fruitful mead ;
Under His guidance I will go
　　Where rills of consolation flow."

Mr. Skurray, encouraged by a favourable review, in the *Church of England Quarterly*, of some specimens of his metrical Psalms, published the whole version, that "perchance some few of them might not be deemed unworthy of incorporation with other compositions, if ever the contemplated selection should be made in order to constitute a system of National Psalmody."

Forty-five of Mr. Skurray's Psalms first appeared in a volume of poetry, entitled " The Shepherd's Garland," published by him in 1832.

E. FEILDE.

1844.—The Psalms of David Metrically Paraphrased for the Inmates of the Cottage. By a Cambridge Master of Arts. Dedicated to the Inhabitants of Rock and Rennington, by their sincere Friend and Pastor. London, Whittaker and Co.—*Brit. Mus. Lib.*

I.

" Blest is he who shuns the way
　　Ungodly men would have him take ;
Where sinners meet will never stay,
　　Nor friendship with a scoffer make."

XXIII.

" As is the shepherd to the sheep,
　　So is the Lord to me ;
From serious harm He will me keep,
　　And all my wants foresee."

Dr. Cotton attributes this version to the Rev. E. Feilde. Mr. W. L. Taylor's copy has on the fly-leaf " To Mrs. Coleridge, with Mrs. Feilde's affectionate love."

THOMAS SPALDING.

1845.—A Metrical Version of the Hebrew Psalter ; with Explanatory Notes. Ward and Co. London.—*Brit. Mus. Lib.*

I.

" Blest is the man who doth not stray
　　In paths wherein the ungodly meet ;
Nor standeth in the sinner's way,
　　Nor sitteth on the scorner's seat."

XXIII.

" The Lord, my Shepherd, will supply
My every want, I know;
He makes me in green pastures lie
Where quiet waters flow."

"The sacred text has been adhered to as closely as possible, from a conviction that, as no paraphrase of the Psalms is necessary for the Christian's private devotion, so neither can it be necessary for any other act of worship. . . . Should the study of the following pages afford pleasure and instruction to any, enabling them better to understand and more fully to appreciate this portion of sacred Scripture, the author will feel abundantly recompensed " (Preface).

Mr. Thomas Spalding, born in 1805, died in 1887, was a member of a well-known firm of wholesale stationers in Drury Lane. He is remembered for his unostentatious liberality among the Congregationalists.

JOSEPH IRONS.

1847.—Judah. The Book of Psalms paraphrased in Spiritual Songs for Public Worship. Composed by Joseph Irons. London, sold at the Author's House, Camberwell.—*Brit. Mus. Lib.*

I.

" Blest is the man (and who is he)
That is from sin and sinners free?
'Tis Christ, the God-man, Christ the Lord !
O, be His holy name ador'd,
He did the scorner's seat abhor,
Yea, He delighted in God's law."

XXIII.

" I shall not in want be pining,
    For my heavenly Shepherd feeds ;
In His pastures I'm reclining,
    By still waters Jesus leads."

Mr. Irons was a Calvinistic Minister of Grove Chapel, Camberwell. Dating from his house, called " Shepherd's Tent," he says that all attempts at metrical Psalms "appeared to him to be unsatisfactory. I have therefore ventured to cast my mite into the vast store of Psalmody already existing ; though I have previously written 611 original hymns for the use of the people of my charge." He trusts " that Socinians, Arians, and Arminians will find no music here for their falsehoods."

BENJAMIN THO. HALCOTT COLE.

1847.—The Psalms of David : a New Metrical Version. By the Rev. Benjamin T. H. Cole, Rector of Warbleton, Sussex, and sometime Fellow of Magdalen College, Cambridge. London, Seeleys.—*Brit. Mus. Lib.*

I.

" How blest the man, who never strays
    Where impious counsels guide ;
Who never stands in sinners' ways,
    Nor sits by scoffers' side ! "

XXIII.

" My Shepherd is the Lord Most High ;
    And He will all my wants supply,
Make me in pastures green repose,
    Lead near a stream that gently flows."

All except forty-five of the Psalms are in simple measures. The deviations from the Bible versions are printed in italics, and the authority for the deviation is given at the bottom of the page.

W. H. B.

1848.—An Entirely New Metrical Version of the Psalms, written for the Music in Common Use. By W. H. B. London, John Rodwell, New Bond Street.—*Brit. Mus. Lib.*

I.

"Blessed is he who shunneth paths
　　Ungodly sinners haunt;
Who flieth when the lips of pride
　　With senseless scoffing vaunt."

XXIII.

"The Lord Himself my Shepherd is,
　　My soul shall never need;
He shall with heavenly nutriment
　　The rising impulse feed."

"He has sought throughout to develop Christian doctrines as much as fidelity to the original would allow, and they will be found in strict accordance with those maintained by the Church of England" (Preface).

SAMUEL McCLURE.

1850.—The Psalms of David, and Song of Solomon, in Metre. By Samuel McClure. Lewistown, Pennsylvania.—*Philadelphia Library.*

I.

"Blest is the man who will not sit
   With men that sinners are,
Who hates the den where atheists meet,
   And shuns the scoffer's chair."

XXIII.

"The Lord Himself my Shepherd is,
   I shall be well supplied;
His tender care and sovereign grace
   Will be my guard and guide.
He leads me where salvation flows,
   To banquet on His love,
Where sweet celestial pasture grows,
   And living waters move."

"But I must particularly acknowledge my indebtedness to God alone, in enabling me to accomplish the following work, which I denominate my profession of faith in Christ. I believe that an avowal of my religious sentiments to the world is an indispensable duty (not on me alone, but upon all professing Christians who name the Name of Christ with reverence, and who place their hope and confidence in Him alone as their Surety), and to make a written profession of our faith in Him according to the abilities God has given us, seems also to be a duty, giving to a sovereign God all the glory."

MORRIS WILLIAMS.

1850.—Y Psallwyr neu Lyfr y Psalmau : wedi ei gyfieithu a'r gyfan-soddi o'r newydd ar fesur cerdd. Gan Morris Williams, M.A., Periglor Amlwch, Mon. Llundain, H. Hughes, St. Martin's-le-Grand.—*Sion College Library.*

I.

" Gwyn fyd y gwr ni rodia 'n ol
   Drwg gyngor annuwiolion ffol ;
   Ni saif yn ffordd rhai drwg eu bryd,
   Nid eisté 'mhlith gwatwarwŷr byd."

XXIII.

" Fy Nuw yw Bugail f'enaid gwan,
   Byth ni ddaw eisiau ar fy rhan ;
   Gorwedd a gaf mewn porfa fras
   Ger dyfroedd tawel peraidd flas."

" The Rev. Morris Williams (*Nicander*) was born in 1810. When about seventeen years of age he came to notice through a poetical curiosity, a metrical ode made up entirely of Biblical proper names. He afterwards became a distinguished bard and adjudicator at the *Eisteddfodau.* He published a volume of sacred verse entitled ' The Church's Year' (*Y Flwyddyn Eglwysig*), in the interests of the High Church revival. His ' Psalter' has taken only a secondary place among Welsh versions. It is fluent and smooth, but lacks strength and fervour " (Rev. H. Elvet Lewis).

FREDERIC FYSH.

1850.—A Lyrical Version of the Psalms.   By the Rev. Frederic Fysh,
M.A.   London, Seeleys.—*Brit. Mus. Lib.*

I.

"O happy the man who walks not
In the counsel of the wicked ;
Nor stands in the way of sinners ;
Nor sits on the seat of scorners ! "

XXIII.

"Jehovah is my Shepherd :
I want for nothing.
He makes me to lie down in green pastures,
He tends me beside still waters."

Mr. Fysh was the author of " Anastasis Examined."
He says, in his preface, " A lyrical measure without
rhyme is obviously the only measure which can
secure a literal and metrical version.   The absence
of rhyme and the indefinite length of each line do
away with the necessity of omission on the one hand,
and addition on the other.   All Procrustean violence
is avoided, and each hemistich is left, so to speak,
to choose its own metre.   This measure is adopted
in the present translation."

M. MONTAGU.

1851.—The Psalms in a New Version.   Fitted to the Tunes used in
Churches : with Notes on Examination of the Difficult Pas-
sages.   By M. Montagu.   London, Hatchard.—*Brit. Mus.
Lib.*

I.

"How blest is he, that doth not in
  The ungodly's counsel walk,
Nor stand with those.that follow sin,
  Nor sit where scoffers talk!"

XXIII.

"The Lord my Shepherd is and Guide,
  He teaches me my track;
With Him I need me nought provide,
  With Him I nought shall lack.
He in green pastures makes me feed,
  Where herb abundant grows;
He by clear waters does me lead,
  Where comfort ever flows."

Montagu was a lieutenant in the Royal Navy, and a sonnet-writer.

"This version is merely the Psalms put into verse for singing, and 'Fitted to the Tunes used in Churches;' just what was designed by the Old Version" (Preface).

A LAYMAN.

1853.—The Book of Psalms Translated into English Verse, from the
    Original Hebrew, compared with the Ancient Versions. By
    a Layman.   London, Rivingtons.—*Brit. Mus. Lib.*

I.

"Happy the man, that walketh not
  Where the ungodly meet;
Nor in the path of sinners stands;
  Nor sits in scoffers' seat."

XXIII.

> "The Lord, my Shepherd, doth me feed
> I shall not therefore suffer need.
> In meadows green He makes me lie,
> Tends me refreshing waters by."

Slightly altered versions were published in 1858 and 1868. The author lays down the rule that a metrical version ought to be literal rather than paraphrastic.

"The former edition of this work, which was published a few years ago, contained a translation, made as close as the laws of verse would allow, to the received Masoretic text. Further investigation has led the author to believe, that this text does not perfectly represent the original autograph of the Sacred Writings, but that the points and accents, although entitled to much respect, are destitute of Divine authority, and that the various readings from the collated manuscripts, and especially the Ancient Versions, must be consulted and compared with the Hebrew, in order to arrive at both the pure fount and right sense of the Old Testament Scriptures. On this principle," the author says, "he has revised the translation."

Altered verse of the first Psalm—

> "Blessed the man, who doth not stray
> Where godless counsels guide ;
> Who standeth not in sinners' way,
> Nor scorners sits beside."

ABNER JONES.

1854.—The Psalms of David rendered into English Verse of Various
Measures, Divided according to their Musical Cadences, and
Comprised in their own Limits ; in which their responsive
lines are kept unbroken, the devout and exalted sentiments,
with which they everywhere abound, expressed in their own
familiar and appropriate language, and the graphic imagery,
by which they are rendered vivid, preserved entire. By
Abner Jones, Professor of Music. New York, Mason
Brothers, 23, Park Row.—*Brit. Mus. Lib.*

I.

" How blest is he in heart and hand,
    Who does not walk with impious feet,
  Nor in the way of sinners stand,
    Nor with the scoffer take his seat ! "

XXIII.

" The Lord makes grants for all my wants,
    And He, my Shepherd, feeds me ;
  He gives repose, where pasture grows,
    And by still waters leads me."

The author claims to have kept closer to the
original in the compass of his verses, and makes the
following comparisons :—

" The Book of Psalms, according to Dr. Kennicot's
Hebrew Bible, contains 5280 lines ; according to
Grabe's Septuagint, 5278 lines ; and according to
Nourse's English paragraph Bible, about 5340 lines ;
omitting 23 for Hallelujahs.

" One version of each Psalm in this work makes

N

5338 lines; one version of each by Rouse (Scottish Ch.) makes 8340 lines; one of each by Tate and Brady (Epis. Ch.) makes 8632 lines. Dr. Watts composed upon those parts of the Psalms he selected to versify about 9500 lines, exceeding by 272 the compass of the present volume, which embraces 286 versions.

"The 119th Psalm contains 352 lines, which are divided by the Hebrew alphabet into 22 equal parts of 16 lines each. In the present work, each part of 16 lines is rendered into 4 stanzas containing 16 lines, as found in the original. Rouse rendered each part of 16 lines into 6 stanzas containing 24 lines, increasing their original number by one-half; Tate and Brady rendered each part of 16 lines into 8 stanzas, containing 32 lines, doubling their original number; Dr. Watts says, 'I have collected and disposed of the most useful verses under 18 different heads, and have formed a divine song on each one of them. But the verses are much transposed to attain some degree of connection.' This shows that he did not pretend to versify the whole; yet he composed upon it 412 lines, exceeding by 60 its original number."

EDWARD CHURTON.

1854.—The Book of Psalms in English Verse and in Measures suited for Sacred Music. By Edward Churton, M.A., Archdeacon of Cleveland. London, John Henry Parker.—*Brit. Mus. Lib.*

I.

" Blest is the man who ne'er hath stray'd
    Where godless counsels guide,
Nor stood in sinners' path, nor sat
    With scornful sons of pride."

XXIII.

" My Shepherd is the gracious Lord,
    Amidst His flock I feed ;
While I am His, and He is mine,
    I cannot suffer need."

He was born in 1800, died in 1874. This version was called " The Cleveland Psalter," and contains a very valuable Preface.

" Following the ancient models, it [the translation] aims to be a Metaphrase rather than a Paraphrase of the Psalms, observing the caution of the ingenious Robert Boyle, ' Paraphrases, though handsome, do as much wrong the Holy Scriptures, as a mixture of silver, though no ignoble metal, does wrong an ingot of gold.' The variation of phrase and order has been made with no other view, than to express the meaning of the sacred text in the language of the English people, and in the rhythm and flow of English poetry " (Preface).

GEORGE TYLER TOWNSEND.

1856.—Solatia Senectutis, or the Book of Psalms, shewing the Probable Origin, the leading Idea, and the Inference suggested by each Psalm, versified in various metres. By the author of " Flowers from the Garden of the Church." Andrews, Durham.—*Mr. W. L. Taylor's Collection.*

I.

" In the midst of the Garden too stood the Tree
    Of Life, to prove both to thee and to me
    That the Psalms appear, the midmost page
    Of the book that declares to youth and to age
    God's blessing on him whom nor hope nor fear,
    Nor the worldling's frown, nor the sceptic's sneer,
    Nor example moves, nor false reasonings draw
    From his dearest hope, God's Holy Law !
    Nor diverts his reflecting mind by day,
    Nor even by night, from the sacred lay.
    He, like that Tree itself of Life,
    Above the world's cares, storms, and strife,
    On earth unwithering, forth shall bring
    The fruits he would offer to God, his King ;
    And, when this prosperous life shall cease,
    Possess in its season, Perfect Peace."

XXIII.

"The Lord is my Shepherd ; hope, comfort, and peace
    Shall His well-chosen pastures for ever attend ;
    Where from earth's barren sands He bids dangers to
        cease,
    And, converting my soul, is my Saviour and friend."

The author says that his version is not to be considered a new translation, but merely the versification
of ideas after the usual iambic fetters have been
broken. " The several emotions of joy, grief, praise,
prayer, affliction, and gratitude prevailing in the
various poems here collected by Ezra, quoted in the
New Testament by Christ and His apostles, and consequently adopted in its services by the Church of

God, were never intended to be embodied in one general Iambic measure, whether they be adapted to singing or not. The author can only wish for the reader the participation of the same happiness in the perusal, as he has himself experienced in the composition, and enjoyment of the holy labours of the Jewish Editor of the Book of Psalms."

Mr. Taylor's copy is entitled on the back, " Townsend's Psalms, 1856," and on the title-page is written, " Rev. George Tyler Townsend, M.A."

ANONYMOUS.

1857.—A New Metrical Translation of the Book of Psalms. Accentuated for Chanting. An Attempt to Preserve as far as possible the leading characteristics of the Original, in the language of the English Bible. London, Samuel Bagster and Sons.—*Mr. W. L. Taylor's Collection.*

I.

" What endless blessings are for him prepared,
Who never hath in evil counsels shared ;
Who enters not the haunts where sinners meet,
Nor sits, presumptuous, in the scorner's seat ;
But in Jehovah's statutes takes delight,
And meditates therein both day and night ! "

XXIII.

" The Lord Jehovah is my guide,
And will for all my wants provide,
In pastures green His own He feeds,
And by the tranquil waters leads."

Preface : " The present task was entered upon with the conviction that a metrical version of the Book of Psalms could have no claim to fidelity in which the strenuous effort was not made to imitate the sententious and the figurative style of the original. . . . To this, therefore, the writer has generally adhered, but he has adopted no such rigid rule with regard to words and phrases, for such minuteness would have entirely defeated his purpose."

EDGAR ALFRED BOWRING.

1858.—The Most Holy Book of Psalms.   Literally rendered into English Verse, according to the Prayer-book Version.   By Edgar Alfred Bowring.   London, J. W. Parker.—*Brit. Mus. Lib.*

I.

" Blest is the man that in the way of sin ne'er set his feet,
  Nor in the ungodly's counsel walk'd, nor filled the
      scorner's seat."

XXIII.

" I shall lack nothing, for the Lord my Shepherd is indeed ;
  Beside the streams of comfort He my footsteps safe shall
      lead,
  And feed me in green pastures, while He shall convert my
      soul,
  In paths of righteousness my feet for His Name's sake
      control."

Mr. Bowring chooses to employ the "fourteen-syllable verse" as the most capable of accommodating itself to the changing circumstances and emotions of the Psalms. He says in his preface, " The main object I have aimed at throughout has been to alter, in the least degree that is consistent with good English and good metre, the actual wording of those noble prose versions which have been bequeathed to us by our ancestors."

Mr. Edgar Bowring, C.B., was born in 1826 ; M.P. for Exeter, 1868. In addition to his version of the Psalms, he translated two small volumes of German hymns, selected by the Queen, and privately printed for her Majesty's use.

AN OCTOGENARIAN.

1859.—Hebrew Lyrics. By an Octogenarian. London, Saunders, Otley, and Co.—*Brit. Mus. Lib.*

I.

" How blest the man, or old or young,
　　Or simple or discreet,
　　Ne'er stood the reckless crew among,
　　Nor sat in scorners' seat !"

XXIII.

" O Thou ! my Shepherd, and my Guide !
　　I would be of Thy fold ;
　　I would be ever at Thy side.

> Thou led'st through freshest pasture, where
> Sweet drops the rock distil,
> Where fragrance fills the vernal air,
> And liquid crystal pure and fair,
> The smooth meandering rill."

It is difficult to find a motive in the wordy preface. This is a specimen of the style, remarkable for its triangularity—

"If this integral, essential, and invaluable portion of the sacred volume has been accepted, admired, and adopted by the Jew, the Gentile, and the Mussulman, how much more highly is it not, and ought it not to be estimated, distinguished, and studied by the professor of Christianity! It not only predicted its advent, heralded its approach, and prepared its inauguration, but accompanies its progress, promotes its advancement, and shares its triumphs."

THOMAS TURNER.

1859.—A Metrical Version of the Book of Psalms (Rhythmical). By Thomas Turner, Esq., Fellow of Trinity College, Cambridge. London, Rivingtons.—*Brit. Mus. Lib.*

I.

> "Blessed is he who hath not walk'd
> With godless men in paths profane;
> Who hath not stood in sinners' ways,
> Nor on the scoffers' seat sat down.

XXIII.

" The Lord is my Shepherd ; I shall not want.
  On the soft tender grass He shall lay me down,
  There, where the fresh herbage my pasture provides,
  And lead me beside the still waters of peace."

Notwithstanding the beauty of rhyme in itself, it appeared to the author that a rhyming version was not so suitable to the character of the sacred compositions as one which is merely rhythmical.

C. B. CAYLEY.

1860.—The Psalms in Metre. By C. B. Cayley, B.A., Translator of Dante's " Divine Comedy ; " author of " Psyche's Interludes." London, Longmans.—*Brit. Mus. Lib.*

I.

" He's blessed who no counsel hath pursued,
    Of wicked men, nor stood
  Upon the paths of sinners, nor hath e'er
    Sat in the scoffer's chair."

XXIII.

" Jehovah is my Shepherd ; there shall be
    Naught wanting unto me.
  He'll in green meadows couch me, and beside
    Refreshing waters guide."

The author aims " at that truth and propriety in poetic form and diction which we commonly demand in translations of modern classic authors, for the free pursuit of which qualities it declines the ceremonious exactness of prose-renderings, and also the modernizing paraphrastic or conglomerate licence of those made to sing in church or chapel."

W. C. YONGE.

1862.—A Version of the Whole Book of Psalms, in Various Metres, with Pieces and Hymns suggested by New Testament quotations; also an Appendix of various Translations, etc. By the Rev. W. C. Yonge, Henley-on-Thames. London, Jackson, Walford, and Hodder.—*Mr. W. L. Taylor's Collection.*

I.

"Blest is the man who shuns to walk
    Where the ungodly counsel hold;
Nor with the wicked stands to talk,
    Till, in the seat of scorners bold—"

XXIII.

"The Lord my Shepherd is,
    How can I ever want?
My care of sustenance may cease,—
    For Him alone I pant."

Mr. Yonge kept the following points in view: "Oneness in idea; sympathy in feeling; association in circumstances; and change and compensation in dispensation" (!). The version was made in 1856, and the author hoped that a few might be helped to enter more into the sense and spirit of the Psalms through the attempt he had made.

ARTHUR MALET.

1863.—A Metrical Version of the Psalms. By Arthur Malet. London, Rivingtons.—*Brit. Mus. Lib.*

I.

" Blessed he, who ne'er the sinner's path with heedless
    footsteps treads ;
  Nor godless counsel shares, nor on the scorner's seat
    abides."

XXIII.

" Beside the pure still waters, in pastures fresh and green,
  As a Shepherd leads his sheep, so the Lord my guide hath
    been."

ROBERT YOUNG.

1863.—Proposed Emendations of the Metrical Version of the Psalms
used in Scotland. By the Rev. Robert Young, M.A., formerly
Classical Teacher, Glasgow, latterly for some time Minister
of the Free Church, Chapelton. Edinburgh, Thomas Laurie.
—*Mr. W. L. Taylor's Collection.*

I.

" Oh for the blessedness of him
  Who walketh not astray
In counsel of ungodly men,
  Nor stands in sinners' way ;
Who sits not in the scorner's chair,
  But places his delight
On God's pure law, and meditates
  On His law day and night."

XXIII.

"The Lord's my shepherd, I'll not want;
    He makes me down to lie
In pastures green; he leadeth me
    The noiseless waters by."

Preface: "The Book of Psalms is one of great importance, and as our metrical version of it is in weekly, nay, daily use by many millions in the Christian world, it is evidently proper that it should be made as free from faults of every kind as possible. Whether these objects have been successfully accomplished in the following proposed emendations, it belongs to others to determine. If the writer has even succeeded in pointing out what is wrong in our version, it is the first step towards a remedy, for though the proposed emendations should be deemed a failure, if the faults referred to be admitted to exist, it may lead others who are better qualified for the task to the successful accomplishment of it."

WILLIAM MILLIGAN.

1863.—A Revised Edition of the Psalms and Paraphrases, to which are added one hundred and fifty short Hymns, selected with care from nearly twenty former selections. By William Milligan, J.P. Edinburgh, John MacLaren.—*Mr. W. L. Taylor's Collection.*

I.

"Blessed is the man who walketh not
    With men of counsel base,
Who taketh not the scorners' seat,
    Nor can enjoy their ways."

XXIII.

" The Lord's my Shepherd, I'll not want ;
   He makes me safely to repose
  Amid unfading pastures green,
   And where the peaceful river flows."

Mr. Milligan writes, " There can be no doubt that
the English language has undergone a very considerable change since the present version was composed, more than two hundred years ago, and the
wonder is that they have not been revised long ere
now ; but they will no doubt be successfully revised,
notwithstanding the inconvenience it may occasion for
a time. . . . Should this humble effort to bring in a
revised version of the Psalms not succeed, still it may
be the means of showing the defects of the present
version, and stirring up parties more competent, or
even the Churches themselves, to undertake so desirable
and necessary a revision of our national psalmody."

THE AMERICAN METRICAL PSALTER.

1864.—The American Metrical Psalter. To the Bishops of the Protestant Episcopal Church of the United States, this Attempt
to preserve Metrical Psalmody in the Church, and to secure
an entire Metrical Psalter, is inscribed with filial reverence
and fraternal affection.   New York, F. J. Huntington,
Broome Street.—*Brit. Mus. Lib.*

I.

" Blest is the man who will not stray
   Where godless dreams allure his feet ;
  Who stands not in the sinners' way,
   And sits not in the scorners' seat."

XXIII.

" The living Lord my Shepherd is,
    I shall be well supplied ;
Since He is mine, and I am His,
    What can I want beside ?
He feeds me in the pastures green,
    Where I may safely lie ;
He leads me to sweet shades serene,
    The quiet waters by."

" The only valid defence of such a measure as the
disuse of the Psalms in metre is, if it be true, that no
satisfactory version is found in the English language.
It is the design of the present volume to test this
argument." The author, or the authors, extract or
alter as they please, eighteen different versions, and
further argue, " It matters little to the Church that it
knows not, with very few exceptions, from what pen
proceeded any one of its prayers or collects ; and the
name of a versifier of a Psalm is of still less moment."

VISCOUNT MASSEREENE.

1865.—A Metrical Psalter.   Compiled from the MSS. of the late
        Viscount Massereene and Ferrard.   By the Hon. L. P.
        Dublin, McGlashan.—*Brit. Mus. Lib.*

I.

" Blessed is the man that walketh not
    As wicked men would guide his feet,
Nor standeth in the sinners' lot,
    Nor sitteth in the scorners' seat."

XXIII.

" The Lord my Shepherd ; I shall want no more.
    In pastures green He makes me lie,
    And quiet waters leads me by ;
        My soul He doth restore."

John Foster, 10th Viscount Massereene and Ferrard, was born in 1812, died in 1863.

Masoretic notes appended by the editor : " The number of verses in the book is two thousand five hundred and twenty-seven. Masoretic sections are nineteen. The middle verse is the thirty-sixth verse of the seventy-eighth Psalm.

" It remains for me to add this precatory clause, ' May the inspired writings of the sweet singer of Israel, and the pious strain thereupon by my dear brother—who thus, being dead, yet speaketh—be to me, as to you O reader, a fresh means of grace ! ' "

DALMAN HAPSTONE, M.A.

1867.—The Ancient Psalms in Appropriate Metres : a strictly Literal
    Translation from the Hebrew ; with Explanatory Notes. By
    Dalman Hapstone, M.A. Edinburgh, Oliphant.—*Brit. Mus.
    Lib.*

I.

" Happy the man who hath not walked
    By counsel of the bad,
Nor in the way of sinners stood,
    Nor seat with scorners had."

XXIII.

> " Jehovah is my Shepherd :
>   Not suffer want do I ;
>   In meads He makes me lie,
> Of tender grass ; to waters
>   Of rest He leads me nigh."

" The key of the Psalms," says Mr. Hapstone, " must be furnished by a knowledge of the circumstances in which they were penned. And it is only the belief that in not a few cases I have been successful in finding the key, which emboldens me to offer a solution of difficulties, which undeniably have refused to yield their secret to men immeasurably my superiors in scholarship."

JAMES KEITH.

1868.—The Book of Psalms rendered into Common Metre Verse, from the Authorized English Version. With a repetition of Psalms I. to L. in miscellaneous Metres. London, Nisbet and Co.— *Brit. Mus. Lib.*

I.

> " Blessed is the man who doth not by
>   the counsel walk astray
> Of godless men, nor standeth in
>   the sinners' erring way ;
> Nor sitteth in the scorner's seat."

XXIII.

> " The Lord my shepherd is ; and I
>   no want shall ever know.
> He makes me in green pastures lie ;
>   leads where still waters flow."

"It is painfully apparent that the Psalms have of late been forced to give way to the use of the hymns of uninspired men. In the opinion of many the change can be accounted for by the want of a good metrical version." The author, sharing this opinion, attempts to supply the want.

Mr. Keith was a bookseller at Dingwall, N.B.

THOMAS SLATER.

1870.—A Metaphrasis : A Metrical Version of the Book of Psalms, made by Apollinarius, a Bishop of Laodicea, in Syria, circiter A.D. 362. Translated by Thomas Slater, author of "Compendium of Ancient History," and "John's Visit to the Isle of Patmos." London, Simpkin, Marshall, and Co.—*Brit. Mus. Lib.*

I.

"Happy is he who hath not proceeded in the counsel of ungodly men ;
  Nor daring to walk with an emboldened step in the foulest paths of sin,
  Nor to sit down in the obnoxious ranks of the assailants of piety."

XXIII.

"Since Jehovah, who ever liveth, hath cared for me, all my wants have been fully supplied.
  He hath settled me in a green and verdant region,
  And my soul feeds by the tranquil streams of happiness."

JOHN BURTON.

1871.—The Book of Psalms in English Verse. A New Testament Paraphrase. By John Burton, author of "Hymns for Little Children," "One Hundred Original Hymns for the Young," etc. London, John Snow. (1877 edit.)—*Brit. Mus. Lib.*

I.

"Blest is the man who turns away
From counsel that would lead astray;
Avoids the place where sinners meet,
And never takes the scoffers' seat."

XXIII.

"The Lord is my good Shepherd,
Who doth for me provide;
By His unwearied kindness
My wants are all supplied."

"In the present attempt to produce a metrical paraphrase I have not generally confined myself to the literal sense; but, assured that more generally there was a spiritual sense underlying that which was literal and apparent, I have sought to discover that deeper meaning. I have endeavoured to catch the spirit of the Psalmist, and to give expression to his divine sentiments in New Testament language."

John Burton—born 1803, died 1876—was a timber-merchant, of Old Street, St. Luke's, London. His son says that he composed his version of the Psalms by rising at four o'clock in the winter, and without fire, and by the light of a tallow candle, completed the work without interfering with his business hours. He was considered so good a critic that clergymen and others sent their poetical works to him for correction. His little leisure time was spent in visiting the sick and dying; in which labour of love he caught the small-pox, and died of the malady at the age of seventy-three.

WILLIAM REES.

1875.—Twr Dafydd : sef Salmau Dafydd wedi eu cyfaddasu ar Gân: ynghyd a Nodiadau Ymarferol ac Eglurhaol ar bob Salm. Gan y Parchedig William Rees, Liverpool. Dinbych, cyhoeddwyd gan Thomas Gee.—*Rev. H. Elvet Lewis.*

I.

" Gwyn fyd y gwr ni rodia 'n ol
Y drwg annuwiol gynghor;
Yn ffordd troseddwyr ef nid ä
Nac i eisteddfa'r gwatwor."

XXIII.

" Yr Arglwydd Jehofah yw Mugail,
Ni phrofaf nac eisieu na gwall :
Fe'm tywys ger llaw dyfroedd tawel
Mewn gwelltog borfäoedd di-ball ;
Fe ddychwel fy enaid crwydredig,
Fe'm ceidw, fe'm cynnal â' i law,
Fe'm harwain 'rhyd llwybrau cyfiawnder—
Ni bydd arnaf bryder na braw."

Dr. William Rees (*Hiraethog*) was born early in the century at the foot of Hiraethog Hill, near Denbigh, and died at Chester, 1883.

A large variety of metres is introduced in the version—two Psalms, the forty-fifth and sixty-eighth, being effectively adapted to the melody of the " March of the Men of Harlech." The Welsh Authorized Version of each Psalm and the poetical rendering are printed in two columns side by side ; and a few explanatory and devotional notes are added after each (Rev. H. Elvet Lewis).

BENJAMIN HALL KENNEDY, D.D.

1876.—The Psalter, or Psalms of David in English Verse. By Benjamin Hall Kennedy, D.D., Canon of Ely. Cambridge, Deighton, Bell, and Co.—*Brit. Mus. Lib.*

I.

" How blest the man who fears to stray
　　Where godless people meet,
　Nor stands with sinners in the way,
　　Nor fills the scorners' seat ! "

XXIII.

" My Shepherd is the Lord : no care
　　Or craving want I know ;
　In pastures green He feeds me, where
　　The soothing waters flow."

Dr. Kennedy was born in 1804 ; Head-Master of Shrewsbury School, 1836 ; Prebendary of Lichfield, 1841 ; Canon of Ely, 1867. Author of " The Birds " of Aristophanes, translated into English verse, 1874 ;

and an " Appendix of Hymns " attached to a volume of occasional sermons.

The author humbly offers his version as a contribution to the general psalmody of the Christian Church.

MARQUIS OF LORNE.

1877.—The Book of Psalms, Literally rendered in Verse. By the Marquis of Lorne. London, Macmillan.—*Brit. Mus. Lib.*

I.

> " That man is bless'd who walketh not
>   By godless counsels bound ;
> Nor stands in sinners' ways, and ne'er
>   Hath seat with scorners found."

XXIII.

> " My Shepherd is the Lord, and I
>   Shall never want or fear ;
> To streams of comfort He me leads,
>   By quiet waters clear."

The marquis was born in 1845, married H.R.H. Princess Louise, 1871 ; Governor-General of Canada, 1878. Author of " Guido and Lita : a Tale of the Riviera," a poem, 1875.

The reason for publishing was to give to Rous's translation true rhyme. "The use of the actual words of the Bible is alone satisfactory to ears accustomed to Rous's Psalms, and I have sought, in the case of the Psalms translated into common metre,

to adhere as closely to the language of the original,
while making each alternate line rhyme" (Preface).

DONALD CAMPBELL McLAREN, D.D.

1878.—The Book of Psalms, Versified and Annotated. By the Rev.
Donald Campbell McLaren, D.D. Geneva, New York.—
Philadelphia Library.

I.

"What blessings manifold must bless
    The man who never hath
In counsel walked of wicked men,
    Or stood in sinner's path,
Or in the seat of scoffers sat!"

XXIII.

"The Lord's my Shepherd, I'll not want.
    He'll make me down to lie
In pastures green ; He will me lead
    The quiet waters by."

WILLIAM DIGBY SEYMOUR.

1882.—The Hebrew Psalter,' or the "Book of Praises," commonly
called the Psalms of David. A New Metrical Translation.
By William Digby Seymour, Q.C., LL.D., Recorder of
Newcastle-upon-Tyne. London, Longmans.—*Brit. Mus.
Lib.*

I.

"Happy he who walks not whither
    Godless counsels tempt his feet,
Stands not in the haunts of sinners,
    Sits not in the scorner's seat!"

XXIII.

" Lord ! my Shepherd ! Thou providest
All that can my wants supply ;
To the greenest pastures guidest,
Where I may in shelter lie ! "

Mr. Digby Seymour—born 1822—Recorder of Newcastle-upon-Tyne, 1854; M.P. for Sunderland, 1852, and for Southampton, 1859.

" I have said enough to make good the proposition that a translation of the Hebrew Psalter combining the two qualities of FIDELITY and HARMONY is still an admitted want, and that the task I have proposed to myself cannot be open to the objection of being unnecessary or superfluous " (Preface).

" *BEN-TEHILLIM.*"

1883.—The Book of Psalms in English Blank Verse ; using the Verbal and Lineal Arrangements of the Original. By Ben-Tehillim. Edinburgh, Andrew Elliot.—*Brit. Mus. Lib.*

I.

" O happy is the man
Who hath not walked in the counsel of the wicked,
Nor in the way of sinners hath been standing,
Nor in the seat of scorners hath been sitting ! "

XXIII.

" Jehovah is my Shepherd ; I'll not want.
In pastures green He'll cause me to lie down ;
Beside still waters He will nurture me,
My soul He will restore."

In a letter received from the author, who wishes to retain his anonymity, he says, "I look upon the recent attempts of denominations to take to prose-chanting as a silly craze of fashion. What would be thought of chanting prose versions of Horace's Odes, or any other Greek or Roman odes? In common life, when we want a song or hymn, we do not suffer a lump of prose to be maltreated for us; so I think my attempt is in a sane direction, whatever may be thought of its success."

In his preface "Ben-Tehillim" says, "To chant a prose version is an absurdity; music, being rhyth-mical, needs a rhythmical subject; as is, moreover, evidenced by the Hebrew Psalms having an arrange-ment of accents differing from that which is applied to the prose books of the Old Testament. Again, rhyme, while it is unlike the original, imposes on a faithful translator difficulties which are insurmount-able; additions and omissions have to be made for the mere purposes of rhyme. Blank verse is therefore clearly the most suitable."

DAVID McLAREN.

1883.—The Book of Psalms in Metre, according to the Version ap-proved by the Church of Scotland. Revised by David McLaren, Minister of Humbie. Edin., David Douglas.—*Brit. Mus. Lib.*

I.

"That man hath perfect blessedness
        Who walketh not astray
    In counsel of ungodly men,
        Nor stands in sinners' way,
    Nor sitteth in the scorners' chair."

XXIII.

" The Lord's my Shepherd ; I'll not want.
   He makes me down to lie
  In pastures green : He leadeth me
   The quiet waters by."

" An attempt is here made to remove from a noble
version some of its greatest blemishes, without interfering with its majesty or straining too much after
mere elegance, and so to make it more worthy of its
great original, and of its place in English literature"
(Preface).

The beginning of the two Psalms quoted are the
same as in the Scotch version.

DIGBY S. WRANGHAM.

1885.—Lyra Regis. The Book of Psalms, and other Lyrical Poetry of
the Old Testament, rendered literally into English Metres.
By Digby S. Wrangham, M.A., St. John's College, Oxford.
Leeds, Fletcher and Co.—*Brit. Mus. Lib.*

I.

" Blest is the man that walks not in
  The counsel of ungodly men,
  Nor stands in ways where sinners meet,
  Nor sits upon the scorner's seat."

XXIII.

" Jehovah is my Shepherd ;
   No want then can I know.
  In pastures green He'll feed me,
  And gently forth will lead me
   Where restful waters flow."

" If the work can be done successfully, it remains to be done," says Mr. Wrangham, quoting Archdeacon Churton. The author tries his hand, produces one of the best, if not a better Psalter than any of his predecessors ; and yet a perfect metrical version "remains to be done."

INDEX.

————◇◆◇————

The Italics mark the Metrical Versionists.